FIREWORKS

EFF COOPER'S

FIREWORKS

A Gunsite Anthology

Paladin Press
Boulder, Colorado

Also by Jeff Cooper:
The Art of the Rifle
Principles of Personal Defense
To Ride, Shoot Straight, and Speak the Truth

Fireworks: A Gunsite Anthology
by Jeff Cooper

ISBN 0-87364-996-6
Printed in the United States of America

Published by Paladin Press, a division of
Paladin Enterprises, Inc.
Gunbarrel Tech Center
7077 Winchester Circle
Boulder, Colorado 80301 USA
+1.303.443.7250

Direct inquiries and/or orders to the above address.

PALADIN, PALADIN PRESS, and the "horse head" design
are trademarks belonging to Paladin Enterprises and
registered in United States Patent and Trademark Office.

Visit our Web site at www.paladin-press.com

To
John Titus Cooper
1883-1942

Table of Contents

Acknowledgements

The author gratefully acknowledges permission to reprint the following stories:

"The Deadly American" from *Soldier of Fortune* magazine. Copyright© 1976 by Omega Group Limited, Boulder, Colorado.

"Open Letter: To A Legislative Hoplophobe" from *Guns & Ammo* magazine. Copyright© 1971 by Petersen Publishing Company, Los Angeles, California.

"Get Charlemagne!" from *True* magazine. Copyright© 1975 by Petersen Publishing Company.

"Home of the Brave" from *Toros* magazine. Copyright© 1960 by Jim Fergus.

"Inferno on Foot" from *Westways Magazine*, a publication of the Automobile Club of Southern California. Copyright© 1961 by the Automobile Club of Southern California.

"A Rhineland Roebuck" from *Guns* magazine. Copyright© 1979 by Publishers' Development Corporation, San Diego, California.

"The First Race" from *Road & Track* magazine. Copyright© 1956 by CBS Publications, Newport Beach, California.

"Mental Conditioning for Combat" from *American Police Handgun Training* by Mason Williams. Copyright© 1977 by Charles C. Thomas, Publishers, Springfield, Illinois.

"We Have to Disarm the Citizens of This Country ..." from *Guns & Ammo* magazine. Copyright© 1972 by Petersen Publishing Company.

"What Is 'Accuracy'?" from *Personal Survival Letter*. Copyright© 1978 by Personal Survival Letter, Rogue River, Oregon.

"Ballistic Wampum" from *Personal Survival Letter*. Copyright© 1978 by Personal Survival Letter, Rogue River, Oregon.

"Baby" from *Guns* magazine. Copyright© 1978 by Publishers' Development Corporation, San Diego, California.

"Rhodesian Elegy" from *Soldier of Fortune* magazine where the article first appeared under the title of "Cooper on Rhodesia." Copyright© 1975 by Omega Group Limited, Boulder, Colorado.

"Wegener" from *Soldier of Fortune* magazine where the article first appeared under the title of "GSG 9: The Philosophy." Copyright© 1980 by Omega Group Limited, Boulder, Colorado.

Foreword

The most important thing I can say about this book is: buy it and read it. If you have an interest in hard, unblinking perceptions of the real world, you will not be disappointed. If you also have taste, you will be delighted.

It has become cliché to describe someone who exhibits more than one talent as a "Renaissance Man." Trite as the phrase itself may be, men who actually approach the Renaissance ideal of multifaceted excellence are not legion. Jeff Cooper is such a man, and of all his books, this volume best exhibits his versatility. The range of his subject matter, from technical firearms articles to humor to serious fiction is in itself impressive, but the subtlety, wit and unfailing stylistic elegance which each selection possesses makes his anthology considerably more than even the most ardent Cooper devotee might expect. *FireWorks* is an opus of engaging literary merit by any standards.

Like Ishmael in *Moby Dick*, who slept with his nose thrust into the cold to better appreciate the warmth of his bed, I occasionally dine with some acquaintances whose intellectual orientation is stunningly to the left. On one such recent excursion through the looking glass I mentioned that I had just finished reading the manuscript of Jeff Cooper's new book and was greatly impressed by it. "Do you mean Cooper the *gun* writer?" one of my table companions asked. "No," I replied, "I mean Cooper the writer. He is certainly the architect of modern practical pistol technique and one of the most knowledgeable experts in that field, but he is a good deal more as well. He is a professional historian with a Master's degree from California and some of his fiction has the lean, spare quality of Hemingway with, perhaps, deeper insight . . ." The interruption was vehement: "I don't care what his credentials are or how well he writes, the man deals with violence and that's reason enough for me not to read him."

Cooper certainly does deal with violence, on occasion, and he deals with it extremely well. It is, unfortunately, necessary to deal with violence in this world, and to avoid a writer of Cooper's talent merely because he is a realist philosophically and an efficient fighting man practically, would be a loss. My dinner partner began a monologue on protecting baby seals, whales, bats, coyotes, gypsy moths, felons and whatnot before I could get my breath or I might have observed that the soldier/scholar—fighting man and man of letters—is a valued ideal in the western world. Socrates was a soldier as well as a philosopher, Ben Jonson defeated in single combat the best fighter the French forces could muster, and Christopher Marlowe was placed under bond to prevent him from repeatedly assaulting an unscrupulous local constable. Cooper keeps good company and, like other sane men of independent thought, he demands liberty as the primary human right. What makes him threatening to the collectivists and social interdependents is that, unlike many who espouse the cause of personal freedom, he is willing to fight for it.

It seems clear from his writings that Cooper does not relish violence for its own sake; he believes in returning it to the giver—appropriately augmented by the recipient's skills.

In a world where excellence has become increasingly suspect because everyone may not achieve it, where the important decisions are made by committees instead of men of genius, where honest folk are safe neither on the streets nor in their homes and where few are willing to risk the remnants of their personal safety for anything so fragile as a principle or an idea, Jeff Cooper's work is like a cool breeze—or hot breath on the back of your neck—depending on your orientation. Should I turn envious in my dotage, Jeff Cooper will certainly be the primary target of my envy. Until then, I shall remain content admiring him enormously.

Mel Tappan
Rogue River, Oregon
December, 1979

The
Deadly
American

IT IS NOT UNUSUAL for critics of the American scene to deplore what they hold to be an uncivilized toleration of personal violence in our society. Violent crime is not so much the issue, but rather the use of violence by socially acceptable persons in self-defense, in the righting of wrongs, and in meeting challenging situations. Such critics feel that Americans are too ready to ignore the police and handle their emergencies personally; and that, further, this barbarous attitude is encouraged, rather than inhibited, by our tradition.

It is possible that such criticism is well founded. The frontier experience of the Anglo-American, while similar in many ways to that of other colonial peoples, was not identical with it. And with the independence of the United States its people split away in various significant attitudes even from their heretofore similarly disposed Canadian cousins to the north. The westward movement of the United States, as placed in time between the Louisiana Purchase and the Battle of Wounded Knee, seems to have developed a notably violent breed of men, probably more prone to homicide than any other generalized group in modern times. This period is only shortly passed, and its memory is still quite fresh in our society. This memory may indeed lead Americans, more than other twentieth century people, to feel that to be a man-killer is not necessarily to be a monster. While a strongly scriptural culture might ponder the Sixth

Commandment at length, it would be equally familiar with the exploits of Joshua, Samson, David and a score of other Old Testament figures who seem to have interpreted the tablet's injunction as, "Thou shalt not kill, unless thou hast a very good reason."

It may be impossible to prove, by a soundly documented statistical survey, that the nineteenth century western American was a more "prickly" man—that is, readier to kill for what he regarded as a good reason—than his frontier counterpart in Canada, Australia, South Africa, Latin America, or Siberia. There is some evidence that this is so, but it is not the sort of thing that is likely to be recorded. The westerner certainly had a reputation for it among foreign commentators, but whether this was founded upon fact or fancy is at least open to discussion. Apart from statistics, however, there may be another way to investigate this idea. Whether or not the westerner was a more light-hearted killer than other people, if we *think* he was, the ethical residue is the same. If modern Americans are more bloody-minded than other people because of a tradition of violence, the factual basis of the tradition is of only incidental importance. This is nowhere better expressed than in Winston Churchill's sonorous comment on the Arthurian legend: "It is all true, or it ought to be, and more and better besides!"

It is the intent of this essay, therefore, to inquire into the concept of the killer in western legendry, and so to discover if our tradition does indeed sanction homicide to a greater extent than our critics can approve.

Man-killing seems to be the natural condition of man. A large body of anthropological opinion holds that it was the predatory, carnivorous hominid who took the upward path in evolution, rather than his herbivorous brother, who developed eventually into the great apes of today. Be that as it may, men have been killing men, with only brief interruptions, since they have been identifiable as men. Thus some problem exists even in separating the Cains from the Abels. For the purposes of this discussion, however, I shall set forth a concept of the homicidal man—the killer—as he appears as a folk hero, not just as a man who happened to kill another man. To begin, we may discard those hero characterizations which a "killer," in our sense, is *not*.

The killer is not a criminal. There are certainly Robin Hoods in American legendry, and many of them boasted a long list of victims, but such outlaws, while often eulogized as "good boys gone wrong," are more deplored than deified. The Jesse James, the Billy Bonney, the Joaquin Murrieta have their apologists, but that is just what they are—apologists. They feel the need to justify what is generally held to be a wicked career. And the others—the unjustifiable criminal killers—the Harpes, the Murrells, the Girtys, and the Dillingers—are, for the most part, excoriated. In some cases it is hard to tell where a folk hero stands in relation to the law, but in these cases outlawry is an irrelevant issue and the man is a hero quite apart from any concept of social order.

The killer is not an "Indian-fighter." To the Anglo-American, the American Indian was only exceptionally a human antagonist, and thus did not really count. Partly because of the vast cultural gulf separating the Renaissance European from the Stone Age; partly because of a fanatic Protestant Christianity which generally held even a Catholic, let alone a heathen, to be beyond salvation; partly because of the really hideous savagery displayed upon occasion by the Indians; and partly because of a sense of guilt about the obvious injustice of the colonists' forcible subjugation of the native people, the Indian was simply vermin. Killing Indians was not the same thing as killing equals. Thus a famous Indian-fighter might have many human lives to account for, and might be highly thought of as a sort of sanitary engineer, but he was not a killer in the semantics of the time.

The killer is not a soldier. Soldiers normally kill in battle—sometimes with enthusiasm and sometimes with the utmost repugnance. But killing in war is a social duty and not a matter of volition. It is reasonably common for a man who is a veritable tiger in battle not even to own personal weapons when he returns to civil status. Such a man may have killed a hundred times but he is not a killer. Wade Hampton of Carolina, the Confederacy's most prominent "citizen-soldier," felt that, in the course of four years' service in grades from colonel to lieutenant general, he had killed two men with his sword and nine with his pistols, but he was not a prickly man. Nathan Forrest, on the other hand, was; but he was so both before and after his military service. Heroic and sanguinary service in war has always been honored by civilized man. Such honor cannot be considered peculiar to any particular social experience, and is certainly not a unique feature of the western tradition.

The killer is not a policeman. The duly appointed enforcers of the law are normally armed with lethal weapons in modern society—Great Britain being the conspicuous exception—and it is assumed that they will kill, if they must, in self-defense or to prevent the escape of a person who has committed an atrocious felony. Such men *may* be killers, but, if so, it is not a part of their job. John Slaughter and Bill Hickok were; Wyatt Earp probably was; Billy Breakenridge definitely was not. Yet all were lawmen, and all killed many men.

(It is curious to note that a feature of Ian Fleming's celebrated adventure tales is the idea that certain secret agents in the British service, designated by a double zero preceding their serial numbers, are "authorized to kill" in the performance of their duties. This suggests a significant difference in modern British and American attitudes, since it seems evident that any man who is officially armed must be so authorized.)

What the killer *is*, by the definition I wish to use, is a man who simply does not hold the lives of his adversaries to be particularly important, who is highly skilled with his weapons and enthusiastic about their use, who does not prey upon society and usually obeys its laws, but whom it is very dangerous to thwart. Such a man can and has become a hero in American legend. In that he serves himself first and a cause only as convenient, he is unusual, outside of the United States, in modern times. Historically, his counterparts are the Mycenaean hero, the feudal knight, and the Samurai. He is interesting to Americans in that he exists in our immediate past, not "long ago and far away." Our grandfathers knew him personally—he *was* the grandfather of some of us. His spirit lies light, and responds to the faintest of invocations. If we are indeed a bit too dangerous for "the century of the common man," his example may well be the reason.

Discounting the creations of pure fiction, America has a host of folk heroes. These men, like Herakles, actually lived, but, as with him, it is not always easy to separate what they did from what they are thought to have done. It is the duty of the scholar to try, of course, but such work does not affect tradition. Alexander probably did not cut the Gordian Knot, but tradition says he did. The act is true to his character, as society remembers it, and Alexander's reputed character unquestionably affected more men, over a longer period, than his actual deeds.

Therefore, in discussing the character of American folk heroes, the stories told about them must be given a certain weight, even if they are difficult or impossible to verify. The image, in this case, may be as significant as the reality.

Most American folk heroes killed men. A minority were killers in the rather narrow sense of this paper. However, the killer-hero does exist. For a conspicuous early example one may consider the case of James Bowie, of Louisiana and Texas. Bowie led such a wildly romantic life that if he were invented he would be disbelieved. "The deadliest man alive" he was called by Robert Penn Warren (alive in 1835, that is). "By Hercules! The man was greater than Caesar or Cromwell—nay nearly equal to Odin or Thor. The Texans ought to build him an altar!" said Thomas Carlyle. This is extravagant talk, but Bowie was an extravagant character. Details of his life vary according to source, but it seems undeniable that James Bowie was a killer of classic dimensions. One thing that stands out in all the episodes that made him famous is a chilling eagerness to destroy. He was never accused of a crime of violence, but, if he never attacked, his riposte was terrible. Such, at any rate, is the legend.

Bowie was born of Scottish ancestry in North Georgia or Southern Tennessee, probably in 1796. Since he died forty years later in the Alamo—the year Sam Colt patented his epoch-making revolving pistol—he antedates the gunman. He was an exponent of the "arma blanca"—cold steel—which lends a particularly sinister aspect to his saga, to American eyes. Americans do not have a tradition of the sword, though one can dig up exceptional cases. Anthony Wayne and Nathan Forrest fancied it, old John Brown put it to ugly use on the Ossawatomie, and there were of course the creole duelists of Louisiana; but in the main this gentleman's weapon was never revered in egalitarian America. Bowie's weapon was the knife, and in his hands it was a fearful thing. "Many a time have I seen a man puke at the idea of the point touching the pit of his stomach," is the comment most widely quoted on the subject.

Bowie appears on the popular scene in 1817 in New Orleans. He is said to have been a remarkably well built and extremely graceful young man of pleasant manners and good speech. (At this time he spoke French in addition to his native tongue, and by the time of his death he was additionally fluent in Spanish and Comanche.) He was something of a dandy, and affected fashionable clothes when in town. By profession he sold lumber from the family-owned mill in Rapides Parish.

His first lethal exploit reveals much about his homicidal turn of mind. Having become involved in a quarrel with a noted duelist, he found himself challenged and thus obliged to choose the conditions. He proposed scandalous terms. The antagonists were to meet in a pitch dark warehouse, in stocking feet, and armed in any way they chose.

18

Bowie was no duelist—no sportsman—and his aim was not to acquit himself well on the field of honor but simply to kill his opponent. He could not match his man with rapier or dueling pistol, so he set up conditions in which neither was as useful as a knife. A single-shot firearm is a liability in the dark, and a sword is awkward inside arm's length. The intelligent ferocity shown here by a youngster barely old enough to buy a drink (by today's conventions) is either horrifying or heroic, according to the point of view, but in either case it is the attribute of an extremely dangerous man. (Needless to say, the swordsman died.)

Shortly after the New Orleans episode, Bowie and his brothers began to smuggle slaves from Jean Lafitte's "robbers' roost" at Galvez Town (Galveston). In the course of an argument with one of the buccaneers, Bowie and his adversary were nailed by their britches, knee to knee, astride a great log and armed with knives. Evidently someone had heard of the young man's feral agility and thought it could be neutralized. But his arms were as good as his legs, and they were again inspired by that lethal mind. The pirate died where he sat.

These two adventures launched Bowie's reputation, and while many tales are told about fights in which he participated in the next nine years, they seem to be apocryphal. However, it was during this period that the "Bowie Knife" was created, probably by James Black of Arkansas, and probably to James and Rezin Bowie's specifications.

The Maddox-Wells duel of 1827 was the occasion of the next accepted chapter of the Bowie legend. This was a pistol confrontation on the Vidalia Sandbar near Natchez. Political factionalism was running high at the time, and the principals repaired to the scene of the encounter accompanied by numerous seconds, all of whom were armed and pugnacious. James Bowie and a Major Norris Wright, who had been on the verge of armed combat once before, were seconds on opposite sides. Details are confused, but after a bloodless exchange of shots between the principals, a general melee ensued. Bowie was hit by at least two pistol balls and, as he lay on his back, Wright thrust him through the chest with a sword cane. The thin blade was deflected by the sternum without penetrating the thoracic cavity, and as Wright tried to free it, Bowie seized the sword-wrist and jerked his enemy forward onto the point of the now famous knife. He then struggled to his feet and attacked his remaining foes. Here again is the killer's determination to drive nerves and muscles to a conclusion, with no thought of evasion, disengagement or retreat.

This event added further luster to the legend, and was duly reported in the baroque language of the contemporary press.

"It was Bowie, terrible and bloody, scorning wounds, a steel shard protruding from his chest, yet striding, in spite of a crippled leg, with berserk fury into the teeth of pistol fire, animated only by his deadly ferocity, who drove the Crain party into retreat. To the beholder he seemed almost superhuman; a terrifying and invincible Achilles, an avenging demon, the knife he wielded like a modern Excalibur, irresistible against any human defense."

Bowie was badly hurt on the sandbar, and his slow convalescence is held by Wellman to have been the proximate cause of his next encounter. His weakened condition may well have seemed providential to a certain Natchez bravo with a knife reputation of his own, for Bowie was a famous man by this time—perhaps too frightening to be tackled when well, but a valid trophy even if taken at a disadvantage. It was only months after the Maddox-Wells duel that the two men met, armed with knives, and with left wrists strapped together. Sick or not, Bowie nearly severed his opponent's right arm just above the elbow. That he did not kill him seems out of character, and this single case of leniency nearly cost him his life, for Bowie was ambushed in a canebrake shortly thereafter and his assailants were assumed to have been in the employ of the man whose life he spared.

The canebrake episode lent fitting corroboration to the Bowie legend. He and his servant, both mounted, were fired upon at arm's length in full dark. Both were hit, the servant fatally, and one horse was killed. As the three attackers closed in to finish off the wounded men, Bowie killed one with a straight thrust from the saddle, a second as he slid to the ground, and then, as the third tried to flee, the famed knife was thrown and landed solidly in the back of the running man's head. As the noise of the scuffle drew men with lanterns, the call of "Who's there?" brought the storied reply, "Five of us. One alive." Here, certainly, is a killer. Fighting in legitimate self-defense, he is by no means willing to let it go at that. The terrible concentration of the instinctive destroyer is such that he will risk the loss of his weapon in order to prevent the escape of a man who is no longer a threat. This is the sort of personality that may indeed repel the tender-hearted, but it is one which is unabashedly exalted in the folklore of the American West. Score one for the killer-hero.

The career of James Bowie subsequent to 1828 is continuously colorful and romantic, but need not concern us here. His death in the Alamo doubtless added to his heroic stature and to his popular appeal, but the figure he cut was complete in the public imagination by the time he left the United States to become a Mexican citizen and the son-in-law and deputy of Governor Veramendi of Bexár. His character in legend stands as cultivated, accomplished, amoral, apolitical, ambitious, efficient, *and lethal*.

If we consider the Bowie legend in connection with that of the other folk-hero who died with him in the same cause on the same day, it is clear that homicidal enthusiasm, while certainly acceptable, is not necessary for cultural deification. Davy Crockett, ten years Bowie's senior, was also a frontiersman, also energetic, ambitious, and renowned. But while he probably killed men without any particular remorse, he had not the enthusiasm for the task that Bowie had.

Crockett's biography, as told in the Potter version of 1865, is almost undiluted Whig propaganda, but it is good reading nevertheless. If it is not too careful with the facts, it is a fine, rich tale, portraying a man it would be a pleasure to know. Since it is largely responsible for lay posterity's view of the man, it stands as "authentic legend," if not authentic history. The Crockett of this legend is a genial, robust, witty, egalitarian peasant. He scorns formalism in manners and in language, ("And as for grammar, it's pretty much a thing of nothing at last, after all the fuss that's made about it"), but he is proud of his rifle skill. However, he does not match the humorous braggadocio of the traditional mountain man in claiming feats of marksmanship beyond the physical limitations of the weapon. He states that forty yards is about his best range, and when he does a good job at a hundred he modestly implies that this is somewhat better than standard performance.

Crockett tells (or, more properly, is made to tell by his ghost writer) of his experiences as a militiaman in the Creek War under Jackson, and while he is present in many small actions, he never claims a personal kill. Nowhere in his narrative does he confront an individual antagonist, Indian or white, in mortal combat. He is a hunter and a soldier and an Indian-fighter, but he is not a killer. The closest he comes to real ferocity is during the siege of the Alamo when he takes a vantage point on the wall and carefully slaughters the crew of a Mexican cannon that has been run up within rifle range under cover of darkness, with relays of loaded rifles handed up from below. In addition to being pure myth (no manuscript is known to have survived the siege) this is the act of a soldier under orders engaged in a desperate defensive action. It is in no sense the musteline enthusiasm of James Bowie.

This divergence in character of the two most renowned casualties of the Alamo is mentioned in passing only to point out that either type of fighting man is acceptable in the frontier pantheon. Of the two, Crockett is the more attractive today. Walt Disney, a conspicuously tender modern artist, could produce a television series about Crockett, but hardly about Bowie. When the most recent cinema version of the Alamo was produced, John Wayne chose to portray Crockett, not Bowie. Perhaps late twentieth century Americans may be softening since the demise of the frontier. And perhaps not.

If there were only one really homicidal folk hero in our tradition, he could be regarded as an exception, but this is not the case. Moving forward into the era of repeating sidearms, we may consider the case of James Butler Hickok, known to legend as "Wild Bill." Born the year after Bowie and Crockett died, Hickok was the first of the great gunfighters, and the only one to make his reputation with the cap-and-ball revolver.

(Longley and Hardin both began their careers with percussion pistols, but "graduated" readily to cartridge weapons as these became available, circa 1875. Hickok remained faithful to separate loading and cap ignition until his death.)

There are interesting personal similarities between Bowie and Hickok. Each was tall, blonde, blue-eyed and notably well-built. Each was conspicuously handsome. Each was vain of his appearance and fond of fine apparel. Each was quiet in manner and neither smiled readily. Neither needed a cause, nor a uniform, nor a court order in order to kill men. Neither was ever successfully accused of starting a fight, but each became famous in his own lifetime because of his efficiency at finishing fights started by others. Each was strong, fast, athletic and immensely skilled with his chosen weapon. And each had a killer's mind.

The killer's mind was more necessary to Hickok than to Bowie, because of the tactical change created by the perfection of the handgun. The knife fighter, and the swordsman before him, usually had time to make a decision about the degree of peril existing in any given situation. The interval between the manifestation of hostile intent and an actual engagement with hand-held, edged weapons was nearly always a matter of several seconds. But with the advent of the handy, powerful, efficient revolver, together with the development of the theory of its use, the time allowed for reaction to a combat situation dwindled to almost nothing. It is very difficult for a normal man to realize that he is suddenly in danger of death. The time it takes him to realize this and act upon it may be, in a gunfight, too long to save his life. Thus the prime quality of the gunfighter—more important than either marksmanship or manual speed— is the instant readiness to react to a threat. This Hickok had to an extraordinary degree, as we shall see.

Bill Hickok was born in LaSalle County, Illinois, in 1837, but moved to Kansas in 1855. He evidently led a violent life as a young man in a violent area, for he was already adept at the techniques of homicide by the beginning of the Civil War.

His first authenticated personal combat occurred at Rock Creek, Nebraska, in 1861, where he was employed as a stable hand by a stage and freight company. The occasion was a dispute between two other men regarding non-payment on a land purchase, and the young Hickok seems to have felt obliged to take sides. There is much contrary evidence as to just what happened, for it appears that Hickok's behavior was something less than commendable, and that, as his legend grew, his supporters attempted to justify their hero by toying with the facts. What is important here is that, at twenty-four, he more or less deliberately killed three men with pistol fire. There is some argument as to whether the three casualties were even armed. This episode suggests a criminal personality, and since the criminal does not qualify as an example of what we depict, it should be noted that the Rock Creek fight was not a comfortable part of the Hickok legend. Later versions turned it into an epic struggle of a noble young hero against fearful odds, which seems a bit overdone, considering the existence of sworn testimony to the contrary.

What is true is that Hickok was a deadly man—an untroubled killer—at twenty-four. The legend makes no attempt to deny this, but rather exults in it. It does try to maintain that his deadliness was on the side of right and justice, if not of law.

Hickok had an interesting, if somewhat vague, war record. He served as a Union Scout in Missouri, Arkansas and the Indian Territories, and appears to have acquitted himself well, though without achieving any rank of consequence. While it is not unheard of to distinguish one's self in war without promotion, it is not customary. A mature man, still in the prime of youth, who serves for four years at the front in a sanguinary conflict, usually has something to show for it. One thinks of the example of Henry Kyd Douglas, who, without formal military training and four years younger than Hickok, went from private to brigadier general in the same war. We may suspect that Wild Bill was not quite as indispensable to the Union cause as the legend would have us believe. However, he saw much action and we must assume that the sight of blood did not dismay him.

After the war, Hickok drifted, and never lost an opportunity to embellish his reputation. He became quite intimate with Lieutenant Colonel and Mrs. George Armstrong Custer, and he particularly impressed the colonel's lady. He also killed, and the records exist. Without going into each example, it is possible to establish the pattern. By 1875, Hickok had become a legendary killer-hero of the first category.

He is said to have practiced constantly with his weapons, and this is not the simple matter with a cap-and-ball revolver that it is with a cartridge pistol. Since percussion revolvers are perilously slow to reload, Hickok habitually carried two. The "Navy" Colt of 1851 was particularly fancied, and this gave him a capability of twelve shots without disengagement. His custom each morning was to fire six shots from one pistol carefully in practice, then to clean and reload, and to repeat the process with the other gun. The advisability of freshly charging a black powder weapon each day for safety is attested by Sir Samuel Baker, the famed British jurist, sportsman, explorer, and ballistician of the late Victorian period. And Hickok was always careful.

His skill became a byword, not so much because of anything incredible about it, but because he promoted the stories as an important part of his effectiveness. It is easy to amaze a non-shooter with one's pistol proficiency, and since most journalists fall into this category, some amazing tales found their way into print. Actually, there is no reason to doubt that Hickok was a fine shot, but his "ace in the hole" was his state of mind far more than his technical proficiency.

Reasonably well authenticated examples of Wild Bill's coldly lethal attitude are not hard to find. The Dave Tutt fight in Springfield, Missouri, in 1865, is a case in point. In this instance the encounter took place at the extreme pistol range of some seventy-five yards. It takes an expert to center a man-sized target reliably at this distance, even under ideal conditions. Hickok, under fire, terminated the action with one shot. This could have been luck, but if so, it was an astonishing example of chance coming to the aid of the bard. If mere chance let St. George slay the dragon, how remarkable that it cooperated at exactly the right place and time!

In the Tutt case, Hickok appears as an extremely intent, deliberate executioner, as the circumstances warranted. In Abilene in 1871, another aspect of his talent was displayed in the Phil Coe episode. Here, before the smoke had time to clear, Mike Williams, a personal friend, leapt up onto the boardwalk behind Hickok, who spun and fired at the sound. Williams was instantly killed. Here is a man who is so quick to alarm that he shoots without an instant's hesitation, knowing that an instant may be a fatal delay.

It should be noted that Hickok was on several occasions a full-time agent of the law, but this need not invalidate the premise that the killer is not motivated by any zeal for law and order or the protection of the public. Hickok was never one to plead unavoidable duty in his homicides, and his tally lists as many killings as a private citizen as in the capacity of a policeman. It seems that Hickok, like Bowie, killed because the act was natural to him, the best and simplest reflexive response to a serious threat.

And Wild Bill, like Bowie, was a lionized celebrity of his time. Not a soldier, not a criminal, not a brigand—the killer was a hero. His exploits were told, exaggerated, and told again. Men admired him, and boys dreamed of emulating him "when they grew up." Score two for the killer-hero.

It is not, to my knowledge, possible to go on and on in this vein, but that is not necessary to make the point, which is that an enthusiastic homicide is an acceptable figure in the American tradition. There are many other very deadly personalities who hold high places in our historic esteem. In addition to a number of frontier characters, we may even list John Paul Jones, who brained, with his pistol butt, a sailor who advocated surrendering the Bonhomme Richard. (Presumably he might have stopped the man by less decisive means.) And, on the other hand, we have a great many heroes who, far from being killers, are positively gentle. The fact remains that in our tradition, murderousness is not a bar to glory, as some might wish it were.

The pertinent question is whether or not this acceptance—even adulation—of the killer is either unique to the American tradition or more evident therein than in other modern cultures. There is always the possibility that the apparent absence of this quality in other bodies of legend is due simply to a lack of a deep command of them. Certainly Zapata seems murderous enough in the folklore of Mexico, and Stalin may eventually appear heroic in the minds of future generations of Russians, but politicians and revolutionists are generally considered to act from altruistic motive, no matter how ghastly the results of these acts may be, so they do not really count. The arresting thing about the American killer-hero is an intense individualism, asocial rather than anti-social, and yet not criminal. In this light his counterpart is not readily to be found elsewhere. When the English Lawrence, for example, found himself coming to enjoy the killing of men, he was horrified. This problem did not trouble the contemporary and equally adventurous American, Burnham. If there are folk heroes in other cultural contexts who parallel Bowie and Hickok, they seem to have avoided translation. If they exist, they must be very minor figures.

It seems more probable that they do not exist, and that one element of the unique American frontier experience is truly a homicidal bent, which naturally leads to the acceptance of personal violence as a natural hazard of life, like death and taxes.

It may be that today the tradition of violence has been driven to the hills, so to speak. Certainly it seems more alive in the West (outside of the great cities) than in the East, and more rural than urban. It must not be confused with the incidence of violent crime, for to be socially acceptable the violent man must be morally, if not legally, in the right. The criminal homicides of the big cities rarely meet with resistance in kind (except from an occasional spunky storekeeper who has had reason to expect trouble and has consequently armed himself). But it may be suggested that the eastern urban population is less affected by the frontier tradition than the western rural element, and that immigrant populations that do not share in that tradition tend to gravitate toward our great urban centers. In any case, it is considered a criminal act to go openly armed in New York or Pennsylvania, whereas it is not in Texas or Arizona.

The tradition of personal violence may eventually die out, as the entire world becomes urbanized, the frontier memory fades farther and farther into the remote past, and the individualist becomes an anachronism. Some will not be sorry to see it go, but there are those who would prefer violence, if it is the price which must be paid for individual liberty, to tranquility, if that may only be had at the cost of freedom. Certainly the fighting bull is a more esthetically satisfying creature than the domestic ox, as the falcon is nobler than the chicken. No man lives forever, and the choice is not between being a live coward or a dead hero, for both will be dead when the tale is finally told. Thus it may be that residual prickliness of the western American may not be an entirely bad thing, nor something we need apologize for. The warning that he who lives by the sword shall perish by the sword may have frightened its authors, but it would hardly deter a Viking, and neither does it dismay the inheritor of the tradition of the American frontier.

2

The Man
Who Knew
How It Was

BILLY THREW THE SWITCH as the commercial began, and the rectangle of light shrank magically and vanished. I hadn't visited my sister's household for the duration of a rather long tour in Japan, and her oldest son had grown during my absence into a fairly worldly young man, absorbed in such things as bicycles, basketball, bubble-gum—and westerns.

"Wasn't that neat, Uncle Ted? Bull Jordan is my favorite program. I bet he's the fastest gun ever. Bet he could beat Longhorn, even!" Billy had the various TV heroes catalogued with that facile precision of the young mind that has been trained to memorize before it has learned to think.

There was apparently a break in the close-knit schedule of afternoon horse operas, giving me a chance to talk to my stranger-nephew for at least half an hour. He selected an apple from the fruit bowl and I lit my pipe.

"How do you mean 'beat,' Billy?" I asked. "Aren't both of them lawmen? They'd hardly want to fight each other with so many bad guys around."

"Oh, you know, Uncle Ted. A fast gun always likes to outdraw anybody else who's fast, too, just to show he's fastest. That's the way it is."

"Is it, now? And what happens then? I mean, do they just draw, or do they have to kill each other, too?"

FireWorks

"Well, golly, the guy who's fastest doesn't *have* to shoot, I guess. Or sometimes he just shoots the other guy in the arm or something. Like the other night. These two guys were friends, see, but they both . . ."

"Hold on a minute, Billy, ol' hoss. When do you suppose all this happened?"

"The other night, like I said. Tuesday, I guess."

"No, I mean when in time. Did all this gunfighting happen last year, or before you were born, or before I was born, or just when?"

"Oh, a long time ago, Uncle Ted. I guess maybe a hundred years ago, don't you think?"

"As it happens, Billy, I don't have to think, I know."

"Golly! You can't be that old!"

"No, not me—though I have used a pistol for keeps—but I heard about it from somebody who really *was* a gunfighter. Did you ever hear of Kid Martin?"

"Kid Martin? Why, he was a real live fast gun. I mean he was a real person, wasn't he?"

"That's right. I see you've actually picked up a little history along with your commercials. Kid Martin was a real person. He was young, stupid, and tough. What we'd call a juvenile delinquent today. But he was also brave and a fine athlete—and killing a man came easy to him. A lot of people were afraid of him. But some were not. He was killed when he was twenty-three years old. You know who killed him?"

"Uh—I kind of remember. They had that on the Rod Rimrock program. Some sheriff or marshal or something."

"His name was John Ellis Longworth. They called him 'Long John.' He was a relative of yours."

This information was received in stunned silence. The intrusion of reality into the world of abstract, electronic adventure took a while to appreciate. I continued.

"Long John Longworth was my—and your mother's—great uncle. That makes him your great, great uncle. He was sheriff of Victorio County, where Kid Martin was killed, for nine years after the Kid died. It was his taking the Kid that got him elected, since his predecessor had been shot in that affair."

"Gosh, Uncle Ted, is he still alive?"

"No, but he hasn't been dead so very long. After he quit sheriffing to join up with Teddy Roosevelt's Rough Riders, he stayed in the army for the fighting in the Philippines. He was one of the officers who persuaded the army to go back to a 45 caliber sidearm after they had adopted the 38, on the basis of several close-up brawls with Moros. He was always a gunman, and he knew more about handguns than most.

"He was overage for the First World War, so he sat it out on your grandfather's ranch up at Mono Lake. You've been up there, haven't you?"

"Oh sure. We were up at Grandad's last summer for two weeks. It was pretty nice—but there's no TV."

"What a shame! What did you possibly find to do for two whole weeks?"

"Well, I did . . . Uncle Ted, you're ranking me again!"

"Pay it no mind, Billy. We old codgers just don't adapt well to the age of miracles.

28

"But back to your Uncle Long John. He died up at the Mono place in 1933. He claimed he was just hanging on long enough to see prohibition repealed. I believe he was about 82 years old, since he claimed he was ten when the Civil War broke.

"He always was a great whiskey drinker, and prohibition was a sore point with him. Not that it hindered his drinking much—his gallon jugs were racked up under his cabin like firewood—but it bothered him not to be able to shoot the breeze in saloons. He was one of the better talkers."

Billy thought I was getting off the subject. He had now accepted the idea of being related to a famous gunfighter, and anything not related to gunfighting was obviously superfluous.

"Boy, I'll bet he was lightning fast on the draw!" he said. "He must have been, if he got Kid Martin."

"Well, you know, I had always assumed that he was. When I was a boy we read a lot about the gunfighting days of the Old West, and even then this idea of 'duelling from the leather' was beginning to be romanticized. You will find it hard to believe, but there was no TV then, so we had to read about such things. There were movies, of course. A lot of those you see now on TV were made then, only I saw them in a neighborhood theater, on Saturday afternoons, for 15 cents.

"So I always thought that Uncle Long John was a quick-draw artist. My father told me about him, but discouraged his children from associating too closely with the old man because he was nearly always loaded.

"We lived here in Oakland and only got up to the ranch in the summertime. We'd be formally presented to Long John when we arrived, so he could see how we'd grown, and we'd say goodbye in a group when we left. The rest of the time, while we weren't actually forbidden his company, we were given to understand that one didn't casually drop in on the neat cabin down by the cottonwoods. Long John was said to be writing his memoirs, and didn't wish to be disturbed.

"Actually, I've never heard of his writing even a letter, and after I did get to know him I thought it was harsh to separate him from the kids. He was very fond of company, and of children, and while it was true enough that he got most of his calories from Irish whiskey, I never knew him to show any outward effects from drinking it."

"Well, didn't you ever get to talk to him, Uncle Ted?" Billy seemed afraid that he was about to lose the whole story.

"Oh, yes. I talked to him, all right. Or rather, he talked to me. I told you he was a great talker."

"How was that?"

"I was about fourteen, as I remember. I had a new rifle, a birthday present. It was a new model Winchester—the famous name gave it extra glamour—and though it was just a 22 it could have been a Purdey and I couldn't have prized it more.

"We'd been up at the ranch only a couple of days, and I was out looking for jackrabbits. Mrs. Werner, the housekeeper Dad used to hire while we were up, could whip up a spectacular *hassenpfeffer* from a couple of young jacks. I'd hunted westward until the sun began to decline and as I changed direction I dropped into the creek bed leading back to the ranch house. Long John's cabin lay just upstream from the main building.

"As it happened, I got a shot a little after I hit the creek. The rabbit jumped at my feet and flashed through the willows to my right. There was no chance to shoot while he was in the brush, but he kept going—crossing the creek bottom and bounding up the gravel slope on the far bank. He must have been over sixty yards away, and running, as he reached the top of the bank. It was too tough to try, but I concentrated everything on that shot, and a fortunate balance of effort and luck landed the bullet right in the boiler room. The jack flipped and rolled back down the bank.

" 'Olé!' I heard a deep voice shout behind me. You hear that a lot now, what with all the Latin music and bullfight literature that has become commonplace, but in those days it was as unfamiliar as old Greek. I turned and saw Long John standing by the bole of a cottonwood.

" 'Good shot, boy!' he called. 'Nobody could do better. Question is, could you do it again?'

"I told him, truthfully, that I didn't know. I was a little uneasy at meeting him like this, alone. I'd only seen him before in his armchair by the fireplace.

"Outside, in the open, it was easy to see how he got his name. He must have stood four or five inches over six feet and everything about him was long. His feet were long, his arms were long, his fingers were long, his nose was long. The ends of his grey mustache were long as they drooped below his strong jaw, and his dark grey hair grew long and was swept back over his ears. Though just short of eighty, he held himself parade-ground straight, and his ice-grey eyes gleamed clear.

" 'You're young Theodore, aren't you?' he asked. 'Theodore, "The gift of God." Well, your marksmanship may be God-given, all right. If you could shoot like that every time you'd be a proper gift to a rifle company. Go fetch him now, I'll wait.'

"I scrambled back with the jack in one hand and the rifle in the other. Long John stood still, a mixture of amused approval and comradely interest.

" 'Bring him on down to the cabin. It's just back in here. We'll clean him and save Mrs. Werner the trouble.' His voice was impressive, deep and powerful to match his great frame.

"He cleaned the rabbit at the sink on his back porch, completing the job in a few deft strokes and packing the heart, liver, and kidneys neatly back into the body cavity. Then he rinsed his hands and looked at me curiously.

" 'Well, Theodore, can you come in and visit for a bit, or is Orion's call still strong upon you?'

"I had no idea what he meant, Billy. Orion is the ancient father of hunters, but I didn't know that. I did know, though I was a little afraid of the fierce old man, that I suddenly had a chance to talk to him alone, without my parents' disapproving presence. This was the man who got Kid Martin, and I was just old enough to appreciate my opportunity. I nodded and we went into the living room.

" 'Just stand the rifle over by the front door,' he said. 'Open the action first, though, and remove the magazine. That's it. Always treat a gun with respect, as well as affection, and it will be your good friend.'

"He went over to the hardwood cabinet beneath the gun rack that held his now unused but perfectly maintained firearms. The glass-fronted rack was a center of worshipful wonder to me every time I'd been inside the cabin. To my disappointment he did not touch it, but produced an opaque jug from the cabinet.

" 'A man who shoots as well as you do deserves a drink.'

"I couldn't answer. My mother held strong views on such things, and I'd never tasted whiskey, but it was unthinkable to admit that I wasn't a man, after he had just called me one.

"He splashed an inch or so in the bottom of two tumblers, put the bottle away, and filled each with water from the kitchen tap. He handed me a glass and raised his.

" 'Confusion to our enemies!' he boomed, and drank half his glassful.

"The mixture both smelled and tasted vile to me. But I dutifully sipped a little. Looking back, I believe it must have gagged him to put water in it, but both of us were willing to suffer for our manners.

" 'Well, now, Theodore. Where did you learn to shoot?'

" 'Dad has taught me some, sir, and I've practiced some with Jimmy's rifle. Jimmy, that's my friend. His father is an army officer.'

" 'Ah, yes. But I don't remember your shooting much last year.'

" 'I didn't have my own rifle then, sir. It's my birthday present this year.'

" 'Well. And a good gun by the looks of it. A Winchester can be relied on.'

" 'Uh—Uncle Long John—did you use that Winchester—that one in the rack— when you were sheriff?'

" 'So you can pick 'em out, eh, Theodore?' He turned and walked over to the rack, pleased that I knew at least a little. 'No, not that one. That's a Model 95, box magazine, 30-40. I didn't acquire that until after the Trip South.'

"For some reason he never would refer to the Spanish-American War by its proper name. Possibly he didn't feel it deserved the dignity.

" 'When I was down in Victorio we all used Model 73's—44-40's. They weren't much for real rifle work, but they did fine for a lawman. Later I got an 86 that took the big government cartridge, but mainly to hunt with. The little 44 was the "Winchester" we talked about.'

" 'I guess you did all your gunfighting with your Colts, though, didn't you, Uncle Long John?'

" 'Not when I could help it, boy! Sometimes I couldn't help it, and I had to use a revolver, but every time I felt pretty lucky to come out safe. A pistol is a pretty risky weapon to stake your life on. Even when a man can use it, there's always somebody else who'll take a chance against it—and his chance may pay off. A shotgun now! A man won't buck a shotgun!'

" 'But—well—I thought if you were real good with a sixgun—really quick on the draw—you could take on a man in a fair fight—'

" 'Hell's fire, boy. You've been reading that tinhorn Buntline, or some such trash!'

His outburst startled me, and I was silent. He refilled his glass—to cut the taste of the water—I imagine, turned and faced me.

" 'Let me tell you something, Theodore. "Fair" and "fight" are words you can't join together. A fight is a matter of life and death, and any innocent who tries to play it by rules simply does not survive.

" 'I was the only regular police officer in a pretty wild region for a number of years. I had occasion to fire in anger more than fifty times. Four times I was hit solidly enough to put me on my back. And no fight I ever saw was "fair."

" 'At those parties where I had the upper hand the other men had no chance. And when *they* had the situation the way they wanted it, it was just luck that pulled me through.

" 'A sane man doesn't play games with his life, Theodore, and when the enforcement of the law and the protection of the people are involved, he should be impeached for trying.'

"Long John spoke with such force and conviction that I was sure he couldn't be wrong, but it was hard to rearrange my ideas on such short notice. I was feeling a little rash from my first drink, and much inflated by the man-to-man atmosphere, so instead of meekly agreeing, I argued.

" 'I always heard that Wyatt Earp let the other man have the first draw, Uncle Long John. He was just too fast for 'em.'

"The old man chuckled.

" 'Buntline, again, eh? Not the world's best press agent, but effective. No, lad, it's an interesting idea, but just not true.

" 'In the first place, a man can move just so fast. His nerve impulses are limited by certain facts of physiology. Some reactions are certainly faster than others, but between two good men the difference is too small to matter. If a man ever allows another to make the first move, and both are in good practice, the first man will have fired his shot before the nerve impulse can travel from the second man's eyes, via his brain and spinal cord and brachial nerves, to his hand. It won't matter how fast he can draw, *because he won't get a chance to start.*

" 'So much for giving the other man a chance to draw first!

" 'But this is beside the point, anyway. The fact is, Theodore, that the man who lives does so not because he draws faster, but because he thinks better. Your friend Earp, now. Some liked him, some didn't. Whether or not he was the crook some said he was, I don't know, but he was an efficient gunman. I didn't say "fast." I didn't say "accurate." I said "efficient." An efficient gunman is one who stays alive after his opponents are dead. Wyatt is still alive, far's I know.'

" 'Well then, Uncle Long John, how *does* a gunman get to be efficient? How does he think better?'

" 'In a fight, Theodore, thinking better generally means thinking first. You've heard of the so-called "battle" at the O.K. Corral? An outsize word for a fracas of that size, but Ned made it stick. Well, by coincidence I was in Tombstone that morning. I had some business with Johnny Behan concerning a pair of horsethieves that had headed his way. The O.K. Corral affair happened that afternoon, after I had left town, but that morning I met Earp and I saw him demonstrate the kind of gunwork that kept him alive.

" 'It was hard to get through to Behan, as the little fellow was obviously unable to concentrate on anything but the tension between the two factions in his town. I did what I could, though, and had just stepped out of his office when I saw Earp and Tom McLowery almost collide.

" 'Now McLowery was tough and he was a fair hand with a gun, and he was in a lethal mood, as later events showed, but he was not a good thinker. If you want to tangle at all with a dangerous man, you've got to act, not talk.

" 'I heard McLowery spit something at Earp—a very foolish remark about wanting to fight him anytime. Wyatt may have answered, but if he did it was while he was moving. Before McLowery had got his whole sentence out Earp had slapped him, just as hard as he could, with his left hand—and had at the same moment drawn and cocked his Colt. He didn't need to be particularly fast on the draw, because by the time Mc-Lowery knew there was going to be trouble it was too late. Earp followed up the staggering cowboy with his gun out and cocked, challenging him to draw if he wished. McLowery could have tried to beat the drop, I suppose, but he was so completely over-balanced by Wyatt's sudden, violent aggressiveness that I don't believe it occurred to him.

" 'You see, Earp thought first. He usually did. That's why he's alive.'

" 'Is that why you're alive, Uncle Long John? Did you always think first?'

" 'Partly that and partly luck. As I told you, I thought second on four occasions. Any one of those four mistakes could have been my last, but each was just that—a mistake. Providence allowed me more than most. It is possible, I suppose, for a man to be shot in a gunfight through no fault of his own, but this never happened to me. Each time in my experience it was because I blundered, and each time the blunder was one I could and should have foreseen.'

"Long John lowered himself carefully into his old armchair, facing the fireplace to the left of his visiting sofa, on which I sat.

" 'One of those mistakes stayed with me. When I talk about it it acts up, and re-minds me of my age. Funny thing, but a bullet doesn't usually hurt when it hits you. It's afterward it gets bad.'

" 'Which one was that, sir? Kid Martin?'

" 'No, Theodore, it was years after that. After I should have learned better. I thought I was an old hand at trouble by that time, but old timers are often the very ones who get careless. Of course it's open to question whether a man ever really learns about trouble. If he did I imagine we'd be able to avoid three-fourths of history.

" 'But, anyway, this particular error happened down in Victorio about 1890. A couple of hardcases had tried for the payroll at the Hollis mines, back in the Ascenciónes. They didn't get the money, but they shot up a guard, and old man Hollis was pretty anxious for me to bring them in.

" 'They were not skillful men—few violent criminals are—and in a day and a half three deputies and I pinned them in a 'dobe ranch house down near the border.

" 'Well, we did our duty about talking to them, but we weren't very convincing. They didn't seem to want to go in for trial. It was getting dark so we had to take them—or risk starting all over next morning.

" 'I set two of my people to cover the two doors with rifles—those Model 73's we spoke of—and then took Pete Vomberg and went in. Pete was a German—I think he was a runaway from a good family—and as good a fighting man as I ever knew. We both had shotguns, of course, and we each carried a sixgun as well. You had to have something in reserve after those two barrels were empty.

" 'Our idea was to burn the two rascals out, but it was too soon after a rain and we couldn't get any sort of a blaze started, and it was getting darker as we tried.

" 'The upshot was that one of our targets decided to shoot it out with Pete, why I don't really know. He jumped through the door as we were busy with maybe our sixth pile of damp tumbleweed, and cut loose at Pete's sombrero, which was visible over a sand bank. He didn't hit but he threw a lot of sand over us, some of which got in my eyes for a moment. It bothered Pete, too, for while he got one barrel off, it didn't do the job and our boy stumbled back inside the 'dobe.

" 'This is where I blundered. I just couldn't believe Pete hadn't killed his man. I was sure he was dead just inside the door. So when the other boy took this opportunity to cut out through the other door, he was the only one I was thinking about.

" 'I wanted to make sure he stayed out, where the rifles would get him, so I stupidly ran straight in the near door and right across the inside of the shack, covering the far door with the shotgun.

" 'I deserved it. I didn't even look around, when the boy's 45 caught me just over the left hip. The sensation is something like being kicked by a horse, though the blow seems less localized. I crashed into the doorjamb, turned and slid to the ground as he fired again and missed. He was lying down, offering only a small target, so I shot rather carefully, one barrel at a time. At that distance a ten-gage shotgun is a terrible thing.

" 'Pete called from just outside the door. Told me the other boy was down and wanted to know how I was.

" 'I told him the ball was over and why in hell didn't he cover my back. He claimed he couldn't cover any of me if I insisted on dancing around like a can-can girl without telling him when.

" 'I was shaken and unreasonable, as I told Pete later. It was entirely my fault, and I knew it. That bullet broke a corner off the pelvis, close to the hip joint, and to this day it bothers me. But it's nothing to complain of; a lawman silly enough to be caught like that is lucky to be able to feel anything at all.'

"Somehow the story didn't seem to fit with what I had heard about Long John's exploits. This wasn't the chivalrous knight of the frontier, stalking the streets of the cowtowns, defying sinister outlaws to match him in gallant gunplay. I tried once more.

" 'But, sir,' I asked, 'when you got Kid Martin—Dad says you shot it out with him with sixguns. Isn't that right?'

" 'Well, Theodore, I suppose you could say so. At least the Kid fell to a revolver shot. But it certainly was not any "fair fight" in the sense that Buntline would tell it.

A fair fight with the Kid was the last thing in the world I, or anyone else, wanted. And, while he wasn't intelligent enough to control the conditions of his acts of violence very well, Kid Martin was never known to give any of his seventeen victims any more of a chance than he could help.'

" 'Well, please, Uncle Long John, how did it happen?'

"Long John was ready for another whiskey now, but pretended not to notice that my glass was empty too. One was certainly plenty, for my head was spinning. The sun was now behind the sierra and my mother would soon be wondering about me.

" 'You should be getting in for supper, young man, but I'll make it short. Actually, there isn't a lot to it anyway, but when you think about a thing over the years, it expands.'

"He sat down again with a fresh glass.

" 'I wasn't sheriff then, or even a regular deputy. As a matter of fact, Bob Peel, the sheriff, had only deputized me once before, and then more for the company than anything else.

" 'I liked Bob. He was a cheerful, honest man with a nice wife and two kids. A lawman has no business with a family.

" 'I was always fond of guns, and Bob and I used to practice together, and hunt together, when he could get away. He was a good pistol shot, much better than I, and very fast from the leather. He used to beat the poker chip, and then bet me that I couldn't. He won, three times out of four.

" 'I was running the livery stable for old Doc Rivers, and Bob was sheriff of Victorio County, when Kid Martin came to town. That was in March of 1883, right after the Tombstone boom washed out, and I was thirty-two years old.

" 'The Kid had been run out of Texas, and was wanted in a dozen places west of there. None of us had ever seen him, but we had a pretty good description of him. Medium height, broad shoulders, black curly hair, dark eyes, very white, even teeth and clean shaven. About twenty years old. Wanted for murder, armed robbery, assault, escape, and suspicion of all the foregoing, plus other odds and ends. Reported to have killed sixteen men.

" 'The first I knew he was in town was when I was told Bob was dead. I had taken the five horses we were boarding down to the creek, when Doc Rivers came running. He told me what happened quickly enough. The Kid had ridden in about 5 o'clock and tied up in front of Henry's saloon. He ordered a drink from Henry and made no attempt to hide his identity. Naturally, as soon as he safely could Henry sent word to Bob.

" 'Since the Kid was alone, Bob didn't think it necessary to deputize anyone for help. He walked around the saloon once to see if the Kid had staked out a guard, decided he hadn't, drew his gun, and went in.

" 'Looking back on it, I could see that he did a couple of things wrong. He should have got some help, and he should have brought his shotgun. But perhaps he thought Henry was mistaken, or even joking. At least he had his gun out and ready when he walked in.

" 'Doc Rivers was in the saloon, along with five or six other citizens, and he saw the whole thing. Bob asked the Kid who he was and the Kid told him. He seemed very pleasant and friendly. The only unusual thing he did was to repeat his name—Joseph Dillon Martin—very clearly when Bob told him he was under arrest. He seemed surprised that the sheriff still wanted to arrest him, knowing who he was.

" 'Bob told him to take off his gun belt, covering him at about six feet with his own weapon. The Kid agreed and slipped the buckle, keeping his hands well clear of the butt, as per Bob's instructions. Doc said it looked almost lazy the way he did it. When the holstered gun and belt were free he extended them toward Bob in his left hand. As Bob reached out to take them with *his* left hand, the Kid snapped the belt over the muzzle of Bob's gun, deflecting the instantaneous shot into the floor. At the same time he crossed with his right hand, cocked and fired his own pistol without freeing it from the holster. The shot took Bob right under the breast bone. It's unlikely that he knew what happened.

" 'Martin reloaded and put his belt back on. He told Henry and the rest that he was going to finish his bottle and that if anyone else in their forsaken town wanted to arrest him there would be trouble. He said he would shoot everyone in the room and burn the place down if anyone threatened him from outside with a gun. He picked out Doc Rivers, who looked pretty harmless, and sent him out with the message. And Doc, of course, brought it to me.'

"Long John paused and looked past me out at the orange glow of the sierra. His eyes glittered with ancient memory. I was glad it was not I who killed his friend.

" 'I didn't really know what to do,' he went on. 'I was no gunman, though I *could* shoot. Bob was much better, and yet he was dead at the hands of this young villain. Kid Martin, though a decade my junior, was a practiced killer, while I had never shot at a man in my life. And he was angry now, expecting trouble, and held half a dozen innocent hostages.

" 'My first thought was to bushwhack him as he left town. But which way? How could I be sure after dark? He'd certainly use a hostage as he left the saloon, so catching him at the door was not likely. A rifle shot through the window? Possible but very risky—the windows didn't lie right and he'd certainly keep clear of them.

" 'I considered these things as I ran a little bay mare, bareback, to the rear of the sheriff's office. Inside, the first thing I saw was the gun rack with its Winchester and its shotgun, padlocked with a heavy chain. Bob, of course, had the keys. I started to look for some sort of bar to break the chain when the idea came to me. It's not mechanical skill, nor the upper hand, that wins fights—it's tactics. Bulling ahead against Kid Martin might get him, but it also might get me, and it almost certainly would get a bystander or two. Why fight him? Why give him a chance? Bob Peel, my friend, lay dead beneath his feet, the victim of his deadly trickery. No, Kid Martin would get no chance from me!

" 'I took off my hat and coat. I rolled up my sleeves. I was wearing my heavy, single-action Colt in its regular belt, but I slipped Bob's spare gun, a little double-action Smith & Wesson, out of the desk drawer and placed it carefully inside my trousers' belt in the small of my back, muzzle down and to the left. Last, I found a worn brass star that Bob gave his deputies and pinned it to my shirt front. I should have prayed, I guess, but all I could think of was hate—hate for the man who killed my friend, for this brain-

less butcher who could ride into an unfamiliar town and leave widows and orphans. I
was in no fit state to pray.

" 'I left the office and walked the two blocks to Henry's saloon. I can remember
my feelings well, even now. I was, as you might say, a virgin at homicide, and it's
traditional for one to remember one's first experience. I was not exactly afraid, in the
sense that I feared I would die in the encounter. I knew Martin might kill me, but this
produced no emotion. What I feared was that I would bungle the job and that Martin
would thereby escape to kill again. I was very nervous about this, for though I thought
my tactical plan would work, I was horribly aware of my inexperience. There were too
many variables, too many things to overlook.

" 'It was important to keep facing the saloon as I approached, so I came up the
alley diagonally across from Henry's swinging doors. Just short of the street I stopped,
leaned against the building and took several deep breaths. I held out both hands,
waist high, to see if they shook. They didn't, but my mouth was dry. I suppose I *was*
scared, but not enough to spoil my plan.

" 'I walked out into the street and stopped about twenty yards opposite the saloon
doors. I called out,

" ' "Kid Martin!"

" 'There was no answer.

" ' "Kid Martin, are you in there?"

" 'This time I heard him. His voice was soft and rather high. He seemed to be
chuckling.

" ' "Yeah, Shorty. I'm in here. Just who the hell are you?"

" 'His reference to my height told that he had been watching me approach, but I
couldn't see how. I couldn't see anyone through doors or windows. This was what I had
hoped—he could see the gun in my holster.

" 'I answered, "I'm a friend of the sheriff's. I've come to see him."

" ' "I told that old buzzard nobody comes at me with a gun. I mean it! I got six other
old buzzards in here, and a bullet for each of 'em. And plenty more for you, Shorty!
Shove off!"

" ' "Look, Kid, I know you've got the cards. I just want to see Bob. Look, here's
my gun."

" 'This was a touchy point. I didn't know what he'd do when I reached for it. As long
as he knew I couldn't see him it would probably be all right. I lifted the Colt out with
the tips of my fingers, reversed it quickly so I held it by the barrel, and slung it under
the saloon door.

" 'For maybe two minutes I stood there. It was bad. He could see me, I couldn't
see him, and only curiosity would prevent him from killing me where I stood. I wondered what the bullet would feel like—you see, I didn't know then. Then he called.

" ' "All right, Shorty. Come on in with your hands up. My gun is on you all the way."

" 'I raised my hands and walked in. The tension was over now. Only the problem
remained.

" 'Inside I saw Henry and the five others, all seated in a row along the side wall of

the saloon. Martin was behind the bar with a half-used bottle of whiskey in front of him. His right hand held a 45 Smith & Wesson Schofield pointed at my middle. In front of the bar, on the floor, lay Bob Peel. He lay on his face in a six-foot pool of blood. The two-inch exit hole in his back, to one side of the spine and just above the top of his trousers, had stopped bleeding. There was no gun near him, and looking down the bar I saw his bone-handled Colt, together with my own, Henry's double-action Lightning, and three other guns the Kid had evidently lifted from the customers. Martin spoke first.

" ' "Well, there's your friend. Don't look too good, does he?"

" ' "Can I put my hands down?" I tried to keep my voice flat.

" 'The Kid looked at me curiously.

" ' "No gun, huh? An' no sleeve for a Derringer, an' no hat for the hat trick." He spun the Schofield and slid it into his holster. "All right, Shorty. Put 'em down. But don't get gay. This here iron comes out faster 'n you country boys can think."

" 'I dropped my hands and looked down at Bob's body again. I stepped around to his side so that I faced Martin across the corpse and the bar. I turned just a hair so that my right side was leading a trifle.

" ' "He's dead," I said.

" ' "He sure is. So are three other lawmen who wanted to take me in. It ain't a good idea at all, Shorty."

" 'He was just a little drunk, Theodore. I yield to no man in my enjoyment of the bottle, but this (Long John raised his glass to the sunset light) is not for the fighting man in action. Slows the reactions, and makes overconfidence. After a fight it's fine, but Kid Martin's fight was not over. I was glad to see it, and when I saw him lean forward with both elbows on the bar I knew the game was won. I spoke to him as formally as I could.

" ' "Martin, as a deputy sheriff of Victorio County, I arrest you for the murder of Sheriff Robert Peel."

" 'His head snapped up, and he tensed, glancing quickly at the doors and windows to make sure I had no aid. Then he relaxed and commenced to chuckle in his high voice.

" ' "You're crazy, I guess." He laughed out loud. "What d'ye think of that! A ten-cent cowtown with the sheriff dead and the deputy loony!" He threw back his head and roared with laughter, holding onto the bar with both hands.

" 'It was not hard, Theodore. The Smith & Wesson slid from behind my back in a smooth and easy twist draw. I didn't have to hurry. Martin never saw the draw, just the gun in my hand when his eyes lowered.

" 'I was very aware of his right hand, but I was conscious of his left, too, perhaps eighteen inches from Bob's Colt on the bar top. Neither moved.

" 'I saw no fear in his eyes, only rage and exasperation. Bitterness at having been out-thought—at having made a mistake. In later years I learned that feeling. Then, I looked into his face and, may the Lord forgive me, Theodore, I *enjoyed* it.

" ' "Now, you murderous guttersnipe, show me how fast you are! Wes Hardin beat the drop! See if you can! Go on, try it!"

" 'I didn't know if he would, but I hoped so. I couldn't tell what move he would make, but any move at all would be enough. A hiccup would do it.

" 'But he didn't hiccup—he tried. With the muzzle of that Smith three feet from his heart, and his own right hand two feet from his gun, he tried. A brave and stupid man!

" 'I had no confidence in the little 38 cartridges the Smith took so I simply emptied it into him. All five shots struck fair amidships before the cylinder clicked empty.'

"Long John stood silent, thinking of that grim moment, nearly a half century before, when he had lost his 'homicidal virginity.'

" 'I heard that he shot back, sir,' I burst out, 'that he nicked you with his shot!'

" 'Not exactly, Theodore. I don't think you can say that he shot back.'

" 'But weren't you hit?'

" 'I was grazed by a bullet from his gun, but he didn't fire it. What happened was this: his hand had reached his gun butt when my first shot caught him right in the solar plexus. A man hit there, even with a light cartridge, will almost always flinch convulsively and grab with both hands for his middle. In doing so, Kid Martin actually flung his pistol out of his holster, over the bar and over my head. It evidently landed on its hammer, and being emergency loaded with six shots, it fired the cartridge under the hammer. This one shot creased my right pectoral muscle, as I stood holding the empty pistol, and the wound caused enough blood to make me quite the gory hero. Actually I didn't feel it at the time, and had to be told I was bleeding.

" 'I recall I thought that one of the customers had hid out a gun on the Kid and had entered the brawl after it was over, hitting me by mistake. I was annoyed.'

"Long John seemed to have no more to say. He poured himself another drink and made some remark about its being time for my dinner. He was polite enough, but it was clearly time for me to leave. The vivid recall had taken him back into a world in which I did not exist.

"I thanked him dutifully for everything, retrieved rifle and rabbit, and went home. Later that summer, and the following year, I heard more true tales of the gunman's world from him. I never told my family about the whiskey, you see, as I guessed that this might cause trouble.

"And that's how I know about gunfighting, Billy. I was told by a man who knew how it was."

The young man finished his apple and deposited the core in an ash tray.

"Man, that was a neat story, Uncle Ted! Almost as good as TV! It just filled in between Bull Jordan and Trail Days. I better turn it back on."

The switch clicked, and after a time the screen cleared and the sound came through. Billy was back in the "real" West.

3

Open Letter:
*To A Legislative Hoplophobe**

I SHOOT. *Shooting is my hobby, my principal recreation—my "life style." Since childhood I have owned, used, and loved fine guns; and I am well into middle age. My shooting skill was fostered by my country, in high school R.O.T.C., and I have used it in her defense in two wars. I ordinarily practice marksmanship each week, weather and business permitting. I also pay my taxes, obey the law, vote, own my home, and send my children through college (where, incidentally, they hold themselves above pot, polemics, and promiscuity). I cause no riots and march in no demonstrations, and I ask only that you, sir,* get off my back.

My guns are as much a part of me as my arms or legs. To disarm me would be as to confine me to a wheelchair. You may think this freakish, but there are a couple of million "freaks" like me in the United States. You may assert that the innocent must often be sacrificed to the public good, but you cannot demonstrate how the public good can be served by my oppression. An individual man is individually responsible for his own transgressions, so let us by all means punish the transgressor, not someone whom you feel, in your total lack of understanding, may conceivably become *a transgressor. Get after the criminal, sir, but* get off MY *back!*

Do not try to extenuate by arguing that registration is not confiscation, or that only long guns are "sporting," or that we sportsmen should keep our prizes impounded in some armory, or by any such similar casuistry. We both know what you mean. You just don't like *guns. Very well. I don't* like *you. But let us nevertheless try to live together in dignity and decorum, respecting each other's individuality if nothing else. At such time as I commit a crime, or even have an accident, with one of my personal weapons, you are welcome to my head on a platter. But until that happens, sir,* GET OFF MY BACK!

*HOPLOPHOBE. One afflicted with hoplophobia.
ADDENDUM
(to be placed in your dictionary)

HOPLOPHOBIA. (1966) From the Greek δπλσγ (weapon) plus φσβσξ (terror).
An unreasoning, obsessive neurotic fear of weapons as such, usually accompanied by an irrational feeling that weapons possess a will or consciousness for evil, apart from the will of their user. Not equivalent to normal apprehension in the presence of an armed enemy. *Hoplon* also means instrument, tool, or tackle, but it is the root of *hoplite* (man-at-arms, *gendarme*) and thus principally signifies "weapon" in English derivations.

4

GET
CHARLEMAGNE!

THE CONGRESSIONAL MEDAL OF HONOR is no light matter. In my early-days, young men were taught to regard it as a far more worthy goal than the rank of general or senator, to say nothing of the mere presidency of the United States. Despite the fact that it has since been somewhat diminished by the custom of granting it for a momentary act of sacrificial hysteria, it is still a big deal—something you get killed trying to attain. Heroism is hard to evaluate, and I do not envy the officers on the awards committees, but anyone who wears the pale blue, star-spangled ribbon is an important human being—a person whose appearance on the scene stops the conversation.

I saw it in person for the first time toward the closing months of the Pacific War. A junior captain of Marines, I was just back from my first combat tour—they lasted 30 months in those days—and feeling pretty salty. We all wore two rows of "fruit salad," of the commonplace kind, but nobody in my immediate acquaintance rated anything very grand. Then one evening in the Officers' Club I looked down the bar and there it was—the big one, the pot of gold, the glory badge! The man who wore it was a tall, deeply tanned colonel, with a white toothbrush mustache, who carried a swagger stick in the tradition of the "Old Corps." To my increasing amazement I noted that, below the Medal of Honor, he also wore a dark blue ribbon with a white center, in the middle of which appeared a gold star! *Two* Navy Crosses! Who was *that?*

Someone told me. That was Hanneken. Herman Henry Hanneken. In literal truth, a legend in his own time. Of course I knew the story. I had read it in Colonel Thomason's splendid collection, —*And a Few Marines*. But I never expected actually to meet the man. It was like being introduced to Jim Bowie or Jed Smith.

Hanneken, as every marine then knew very well, was a mustang who had won his blue ribbon as an enlisted man for an exotic and irregular clandestine operation in the Caribbean. It was dream stuff, of a sort to stir the blood of any proper globe-eagle-and-anchor man. It was a simply perfect "spook-show" and it deserves retelling.

This, then, is the remarkable tale of Hanneken's Medal of Honor.

Haiti in 1918 was in the throes of one of those mean little 20th century fights that you can call a police action, or a revolution, or an insurgency, or even a "state of unrest," but which politicians hate to come right out and call a "war." This delicacy of expression is amusing to soldiers, who know you can get killed just as dead in Ulster or Mindanao or Mozambique as you can at an Iwo or an Alamein. The fighting trade is always active, like medicine or espionage, and it was in full swing in the black Caribbean republic at the end of World War I.

It seems that the government was oppressing the people, or vice versa, depending on who was buying your drinks, and the United States was making one of its periodic efforts to damp down the racket so that the various interested parties could sort themselves out. The Haitian gendarmerie was the principal police agency, but in order to lend it a bit of additional muscle, a treaty was arranged by which a number of hand-picked U.S. Marines—all non-commissioned officers—were sworn in as officers in the gendarmerie, holding both jobs at once and drawing appropriate pay and allowances. These were excellent men, for the Marine Corps of that day was a select organization, and these were the best Marines that could be had.

The five essentials of the soldier are skill-at-arms, discipline, hardihood, valor and pride. The Marines in the gendarmerie were conspicuous examples of this concept. But for irregular service another element is desirable, and that is subtlety. As it turned out, this last was most important in the Hanneken episode. Where he learned it is impossible to find out now. But he did, and that is what made the whole thing possible.

Hanneken was born in 1893, so he was 25 in 1918, when this story begins, and 26 a year later, when it concludes. He was an unusual man in many ways, with a surprisingly dark skin for a blond, cold gray eyes, and an aloof, silent manner. He had a natural ear for languages, uncommon in Americans, and an inherent, untutored talent for personality analysis. One does not expect this in a buck sergeant, but perhaps one should in a gendarmerie captain. He held both ranks at once.

When Hanneken took over his company and sector in the northern part of the republic, the principal hot spot lay in the south. There, a certain Charlemagne Péralte— one-quarter French, three-quarters black—had developed into a fairly successful revolutionary demagogue. Not much was known about him except that he had sufficient talent, both as an orator and as a killer, to make an utter nuisance of himself to both halves of the Haitian "establishment"—U.S. and home-grown.

The island is ideal for guerrilla activity; heavily wooded, mountainous, largely trackless, and populated thickly enough so that an irregular force need never lack for food or information. In the tradition of such movements, the Cacos, as the insurgents were called, committed the greater part of their harassments against the long-suffering peasantry, but what they advertised were their occasional successes against the government, and so set themselves up as what would be known as an "army of liberation" in proper Marxist parlance.

As is only too apparent in current world affairs, it is very difficult for a regular army to go after one of these backwoods groups and bring it to bay. You can't tell the bad guys from the good without a program, and unless you are prepared to "concentrate" the entire population into camps behind wire (as was done successfully by Templar in Malaya), you have no way of getting your teeth into your target.

There is another answer, however, and I find it curious that history has been so badly taught that nobody in a responsible position seems to be able to profit by it. Insurgency needs charismatic personal leadership. Without talented local chiefs it cannot function. Therefore, if you want to stop it, you get rid of the chiefs. You don't do this by bombing their headquarters, or by landing paratroops at their rear. You do this by shooting them—in person. In Haiti, in 1918, this was the solution.

After careful consideration of all aspects of the situation, G.H.Q. issued an order: "Get Charlemagne Péralte, and get him in such a way as can be irrefutably proven to all concerned." The order reached Captain Hanneken in due course, and he set about obeying it.

Back there in the southern mountains there is a man. He is not in your zone of operations. You have never seen him, and there are no photos available. He commands large forces, and you cannot pass among them without being spotted as a "blanc." He has eyes and ears everywhere, so you cannot do anything openly. And it's not enough just to take him. You must be able to prove that you have. That means you must produce the corpus delicti for all to see. Any questions? Move out!

You don't argue about orders, you just carry them out. *How* you do it is up to you. Hanneken at least had two special advantages. He had picked up enough of the backwoods Haitian French to sound, if not like a local, at least like somebody from some other part of the island. And he was astonishingly good at sizing up the motives and capacities of everybody he dealt with. He made a plan, and like all good "spook" plans, he kept it completely to himself, letting out only such bits of it to those who had to know, and not to them until the last possible instant.

There was no way he could attack Péralte until the actual moment of truth. He had to bring Péralte to him. What should be the lure? Hanneken did not know Péralte as an individual, but he knew the proper bait for a demagogue—power. Charlemagne was the big man in the South. Doubtless he wanted to be the big man in the whole Caco movement. How would he react to a rival in the North?

Hanneken's company was based at a town called Grande Rivière, which was the home of a local big shot known as Conzé. This Conzé was presumably friendly with the government, but in such circumstances one is never certain. Sides can be changed quickly if a bandwagon begins to take shape. There was a private meeting. There was

FireWorks

the matter of the reward money—$2,000 *in gold;* say ten times that in today's purchasing power—a fortune in Haiti. Very shortly, and quite openly, Conzé defected. He said the Americans had snooted him and he would not stand for that. He split for the hills and set up as a Caco chief.

How he and Hanneken communicated was a marvel of spook technique. They stayed in close touch for nearly six months and nobody knew but the two of them. Conzé was an immediate success. Naturally. Everything went his way, naturally, and his fame spread. Péralte heard about him presently and thoughtfully ordered him assassinated. One revolutionary saviour is enough. But the plan did not succeed, and when Conzé uncovered it he sent a fawning message to Péralte claiming that he had no ambitions beyond the liberation of his people, and would be honored to place himself and his men completely under the direction of the most high and magnificent Charlemagne Péralte. To prove both his worth and his loyalty he would soon take a town—his home town of Grande Rivière—and make a present of it to his illustrious chief, Charlemagne. Of course he would need more men. If Charlemagne could send him some? He did not actually suggest that Péralte come in person. The fish had to be played with a very light leader. But Hanneken felt that if Péralte took the bait he would indeed come himself, both to keep track of his expeditionary force and to be personally present to claim the glory.

Péralte grandly appointed Conzé a two-star general and told him he'd think about it. So far so good.

Hanneken decided that one more confidant was necessary, to arrange for target identification. A gendarme deserted, taking his weapons with him. He also had the effrontery to steal the captain's personal pistol, a pearl-handled revolver that had been the envy of the whole district. He did not join Conzé, but made his way south to the country of Charlemagne, where, because he could read and write very well, he was taken on as the great man's private secretary. He had endeared himself to Péralte by making him a present of the American captain's own pretty sidearm, and he got word back that the Caco leader now never appeared without that notable weapon stuck in his sash. There were no other white-handled handguns in his command. It was his new badge of office.

After three months of nicely coordinated depredation, Conzé was flying high. He actually constructed a strong point, which, incredibly enough, beat off an attack by Hanneken's company. In this action the captain was seen to fall heavily in the brush and come crawling out with a bloody arm, which he insisted on tending himself. This captain was not so much, perhaps. The Cacos were making a fool of him, and now he was disabled. These Americans were paper tigers. Smart money should be placed on the side of Conzé, his Cacos, and the great Péralte, who was now on his way, people said, to Grande Rivière.

So all the preliminaries had worked—amazingly. In war and in clandestine operations things almost never go according to plan. But Hanneken's plan was working. Any professional will tell you that it was too intricate, too wasteful (Conzé's raids and ambushes were real, and casualties were unavoidable), called for unrealistic perfection

46

in communications, and needed too large an element of luck. But Hanneken was not a professional spook, so, like the bumblebee, he just went ahead and flew.

D-Day arrived—the Caco attack on Grande Rivière. Only Hanneken, Conzé, and Péralte's private secretary knew that there was anything odd about it. No, there was one other. At sundown on the scheduled night, Hanneken told Lt. William Button of the gendarmerie, a corporal of Marines, what was going to happen. For the task he had assigned himself, the captain needed a man to cover his back. He then assigned a ten-man gendarmerie patrol, and made ready. He could not tell his company that they were about to be hit, but he made sure that they were as ready as he could make them. Knowing the time and direction of Conzé's attack was naturally a big help. He turned over to his second-in-command, and then turned himself, Button, and the patrol into Cacos. He stripped off the phony sling and bandages from his "wounded" arm. He and Button stained their bodies a deep chocolate brown, so well that it took the two of them six weeks to resume their original shade. All hands got out of uniform and into the cotton tatters of the countryside. Hanneken equipped himself with a U.S. service pistol, Model 1911, and directed that Button carry a B.A.R.—the splendid automatic assault rifle that the Marines fell in love with on the Pacific Islands of World War II. It's a heavy piece—more than 20 pounds loaded—and a burden to pack on a hot day, but it hits very hard, and it always works. The patrol carried a variety of personal hardware, as befits a guerrilla band.

The sun set and the time had come for the final scene. The bull had been played with cape, pic and muleta, and now was ready for the sword. But as the sword goes in, the bull can raise his head, and the horns are sharp.

The plan was to cross the river, take cover, and wait for the attack behind the center of Conzé's main effort. This is where Charlemagne was to be guided to oversee the final assault. The patrol made its move carefully, and, passing as Caco reinforcements, reached its position by full dark. On the way, they estimated that they saw seven hundred real Cacos moving up for the fight.

On schedule, the action commenced. It was violent, as the defenders, not taken unawares, chopped into the attacking waves with well-sited Browning water-cooled machine guns. There was a fearful racket. No one who has not personally attended such an affair has any idea how *loud* it is.

Hanneken worked up to where he could see Conzé's command post, but there was no sign of Péralte. Then they were suddenly joined by the defected secretary, who was in a bad state of nerves. Péralte had decided not to move up, but to "command" his troops from a hilltop observation post a couple of miles to the rear.

There was only one possible decision. At no matter what risk, Hanneken had to go straight in for the kill. Too much had now been committed to try for another time. Good men had died to set this stage. The director now could only offer his own life to assure that they had not died for no purpose.

He had the password, and he spoke the patois. He was dressed authentically and his skin was the right shade. No one could tell the color of his eyes in the dark night. There was no time to sneak in; besides, he could not find his way unless he followed

the marked and guarded trail. He left his men in position as he and Button approached the first outpost, with orders for them to attack along his tracks as soon as they heard his first shot. He and Button went on alone.

There were four check points. At each one he shouted the password and the great good news. Grande Rivière was as good as taken! Our men are in the town! The defenders are running! The Chief must be told!

Gobbling with excitement and out of breath, they brushed past one outpost, and a second—and a third. Stumbling on up the trail toward the hilltop, they hit the last. A man as big as Hanneken barred the way.

"Qui va là?" A pistol pointed right at Hanneken's belt buckle.

"Général Jean!" The captain yelled the password. *"Où est le chef? Victoire! Victoire!"* The two lunged on toward a campfire burning low on the summit. The tall man followed, pistol ready. Button edged between him and Hanneken in the dark.

"Victoire, mon Général!"

A medium-sized brown man stepped forward into the firelight. He wore a silk shirt. From the sash around his waist protruded the butt of a revolver—with white stocks.

Hanneken's thumb slipped upward under the flap of the service holster, flipping it open as his hand socked into the butt of the big pistol. He drew smoothly and pointed, as the eyes of the man across the fire widened in that quick dismay that is the last consciousness before violent death. Hanneken caught the briefest glimpse of the front sight against the pale silk of the shirt, and squeezed. Nineteen times out of twenty, the half-ounce, half-inch, blunt bullet of the 45 concludes an action with one solid hit. It did in this case. The first half of the mission was accomplished.

Hell broke loose.

As Hanneken had drawn his pistol, Button had whirled, and, from its muzzle-down, ready position brought the barrel of the B.A.R. up sharply under the gun wrist of the guard, sending his pistol flying. Button continued the arc of the heavy gun with all his strength, delivering a diagonal butt stroke to the man's jaw. That was that, but the aroused personal guards of the late Caco leader loomed close in the gloom, nicely bunched, and Button cut loose with his piece on full auto, held waist-high. The B.A.R. is no trifling machine pistol, nor one of your latter-day, cut-down "poodle-shooters," such as are now standard around the world. It took a full-house 30-06 cartridge and could drive easily through four, five, or six men, should they be unlucky enough to stand in a row. It played upon the guard squad like a blowtorch on a piece of tissue paper, and its sustained burst started the gendarme patrol up the hill on a run.

Hanneken leaped across the embers, grabbed Péralte's body by an ankle, heaved it into a convenient hollow, and dropped alongside. Button hit the deck nearby as he changed magazines, and both began shooting at any flashes that came from the dark—their patrol having been ordered to attack with bayonets and machetes only.

Howls, curses and shots reached a crescendo, then gradually tapered off. Hanneken located his people after a time, and they him. They were right in the middle of the Caco rear. The problem now was to get out—with the body.

With Conzé suddenly absent—at the bottom of the deepest hole he could find—and Charlemagne permanently uninterested in events, the attack on Grande Rivière faltered and collapsed. Dispirited Cacos straggled rearward, shooting petulantly at anything that moved. Finding peril behind them and disorder in full cry, they split for home after the manner of unsuccessful irregulars.

Hanneken, Button and company were able to collar an inquisitive burro, and, throwing the deceased liberator across him, hit the trail for base camp. This move was extremely worrisome, for they were under intermittent but very sincere rifle fire throughout the whole march, first from one side and then from the other. Nobody, miraculously, was hit, but near misses became so commonplace that they ceased to hold interest. The little group, with its burro load, proceeded much like ducks in a shooting gallery patronized by very drunken sailors.

Matters eventually cleared up, as matters will, and there came the time when the two marines could unload, undress, and wash down, their hammocks waiting. We can be sure that Hanneken was too good an officer to turn in before inspecting his sentries, but the overwhelming awareness of the accomplishment of a well-nigh impossible task, together with the sudden release of six months' tension, probably then knocked him out like a veinful of Pentothal.

Happiness is the by-product of achievement, and Herman Hanneken awoke a happy man.

Charlemagne Péralte was the guest of honor at funerals in various towns in Haiti, but officially buried in secret to avoid the acquisition of his remains for purposes of voodoo magic.

Conzé and the private secretary split the reward, though Hanneken was hard put to save the latter's life as the gendarmerie felt that defectors of any sort should be hanged as a matter of policy. Their captain suggested that it would be very difficult to enjoy a thousand dollars in gold while swinging at the end of a rope, and they finally came around, albeit reluctantly.

Hanneken garnered no loot, of course, as it was not the fashion then, nor is it now, to reward heroism with wealth and security. Both he and Button were cited, however, and he was commissioned a regular lieutenant of Marines, so he could go on risking his life in the line of duty. Which, of course, he did. You do not get the Navy Cross—even once—for maintaining a shipshape barracks or editing field manuals.

But what he did get for his unique display of intuitive intelligence, professional competence and raw courage was that one thing that placed him among the very few whose names will live in glory as long as the human race keeps records. It is a pale blue ribbon dotted with white stars. It is worn around the neck, and from it depends a bronze medallion. It is the membership emblem for the society of valor.

5

The Trip Home

THE SHIP SWUNG AT ANCHOR, protected by her torpedo nettings, in a secluded harbor in the New Hebrides. The war had rolled on to the North, and the island was now a major base of U.S. power, churning with activity directed inexorably toward the forthcoming invasion of the Japanese home islands, a grim operation expected to cost one million American lives—and probably twenty times that many Japanese.

The vessel was an obsolescent battleship, no longer suitable for her original role as a sea-sweeper, but nearly perfect for her new job as an immensely powerful source of gunfire in support of landing operations. She had been hit at Pearl Harbor, and had thereupon embarked upon a new career as a protector of troopships and a killer of islands. She had ranged far and wide upon the great ocean, from the Aleutians to Australia, and no one could guess how many thousands of Japanese warriors had perished under her guns. She was not fast nor graceful like her newer sisters, but she packed twelve fourteen-inch guns and sixteen five-inchers, and wielded them with murderous skill. Each main battery projectile stood taller than a man and weighed 1,500 pounds. No pillbox nor bunker could withstand it. Her crew had fired more shots in anger than any other in the navy; and practice, they say, makes perfect.

Ship for ship, she stood about as much chance against the Yamato as a Stuka against

a Spitfire, but in her proper sphere of operations she was an efficient engine of war.

The men of that ship did not think of themselves as paladins. They were concerned chiefly with doing the best possible job, getting some sleep, and—if at all possible— eventually coming home whole (approximately in that order). Their names were Corn, Martin, Masterson, Burch, Eicher, and hundreds more. They were hard, tired, merciless men, and they labored to exhaustion—month after month—at their unglamorous task, protecting troopships and killing islands.

Their morale was high, but it was not that of a crusade—religious or political. Their attitude toward the enemy was one of scornful exasperation. They were wrong in this, for the Japanese navy was far better than they believed, but they viewed matters on essentially racial terms and they thought of their foes as more presumptuous than frightening. They knew that they, as individuals, could be killed by those funny little men whose dead bodies seemed to run mainly to teeth, but it never occurred to them that they, as a team, might lose even a battle, much less a war.

In his autobiography the great Japanese ace Saburo Sakai expresses astonishment at the foolhardy valor of the American and Australian pilots over New Guinea, who did not seem to understand that the Japanese had better fliers, better aircraft, and more experience. He could not have been expected to realize that those "Anglos" simply could not elevate the "Nips" to a place of honor. The Americans in the forward areas, almost to a man, shared a mood comparable to that of a medieval knight who, while taking his unarmored ease before a cheery fire, had been slugged from behind by a dwarf. The roar of rage was quite naturally followed by devastating counterattack, the object of which was utter annihilation.

Among the crew of the ship was a marine officer. In naval parlance he was *the* marine officer, since he was commanding officer of the ship's marine detachment. He was a twenty-four-year-old captain, much too young for his job but doing it well enough, considering that the United States had eleven million men under arms and could hardly expect perfection. He was six-feet two-inches tall, weighed one hundred sixty-five pounds, and had short brown hair, a deep tan on the lower half of his face, and bright blue eyes. Like the others, he was professionally adept, quite deadly, and very, very tired. He was also unbearably in love with his beautiful young wife, thirty months away on the other side of the world, and his relieving officer had finally—after six months—caught up with him.

There was no "rotation" policy in those days, as far as he knew, and everyone expected that the United States would keep right on feeding men and machines into the war—without pulling anything back—until the enemy was ground into garbage. When the marine officer saw orders to turn over his detachment and report to a training camp in California he was somewhat shaken. The idea that he might go home before Japan was ploughed under had not occurred to him. But nothing shakes a battle-hardened veteran of twenty-four for long, and the idea that he was now only weeks away from his best-beloved darling made him giddy.

There was a crashing presentation of arms (the marine officer was an unabashed martinet) as salutes were exchanged. His gear, including the pre-war luxury of a steamer trunk, was waiting below in the whale-boat. There was a short speech to his men. "You will continue to do your duty as you have done it, and, live or die, you will have reason to be proud." There was a clicking of heels, and the formal declaration to the officer of the deck (a comrade of several battles), "Sir, I have orders to leave the ship."

"Very well, sir!"

Face aft. Salute the colors. Order arms. A hundred rifle butts clang on the iron deck. Face smartly outboard and leap down the ladder into the boat.

"Shove off, Cox'n!" Going home!

Problems are properly approached one at a time. The marine officer had at last been relieved. He had not thought about the mechanics of getting back to America. Now, however, it was time to get into that.

On the beach with his gear, he ordered himself into the presence of the harbor-master, a less-than-impressive lieutenant commander who directed all such spare parts to a compound ambitiously labeled "Transient Officers' Quarters," which had the general aspect of a rather humane concentration camp.

The marine officer was not at all pleased with this scene. He was inured to heat, cold, hunger, thirst, pain, and exhaustion—but not to disrespect. He quickly discovered that once you are on your way home you are a non-person—no longer involved in important matters. People, including some very *good* people, had jumped at his command for quite some time, but now he found that the two silver bars on his collar did not produce the effect to which he had become accustomed. His response to this discovery was—as befits a marine—belligerent. Within twenty-four hours he shifted his personality mode from company commander to gunnery sergeant. And a gunnery sergeant with two bars is a very effective character in the zone of communications of a major war.

Passively waiting for orders to be processed, while censoring endless mountains of mail on starvation rations in a jail-house atmosphere, is no fit duty for an honest-to-God man. The marine officer huffed and puffed and, if he did not blow the house down, he blew a hole in the wall big enough to crawl through.

On the bulletin board he saw an order signed by the base re-assignment officer. The name was Manfred Cantrell. He had been in high school R.O.T.C. with a Manfred Cantrell, and he felt fairly sure that there could not be two men with a name like that. He bullied the watch officer into putting him through by telephone, and it was indeed the same man. Inside an hour he was processed out of the para-prison and installed as a house guest in Cantrell's quarters. By some standards they might not have seemed palatial, but under those circumstances they were. Set on stilts on a green hillside shaded by spreading palms, with a good bed, an adequate bar, and various bootleg delicacies in a small refrigerator, they seemed indecently luxurious. With no watches to stand and no mission to accomplish, the marine officer went limp and slept around the clock—and then some. He might have slept himself to death if such a thing were biologically possible. As it was, thirst finally woke him up.

So far so good. Only important people travelled by air in those days, and when a berth on a homeward-bound ship was located an interval of five days was the least that could be arranged. The delay was not serious. The green, the privacy, and the quiet were things the marine officer had forgotten. Finding that they still existed was an unearthly delight.

On the third night there was a party. Lieutenant Cantrell and a colleague, by dint of ingenuity, chicanery, bravado, and sheer determination, had at long last arranged a "date" with two Red Cross girls. There were about two dozen such on the island and—along with the nurses at the hospital—they became target number one for about 40,000 randy young men of all sizes, shapes, services, and ranks. To arrange for the exclusive company of a real, live, white girl for a whole evening was a feat of shattering magnitude, rather on the order of having the Pope to dinner. The marine officer's presence was naturally not going to interfere. The . . . er . . . *show* must go on.

The girls' barracks was located across the island, about twenty minutes by road each way. As the afternoon drew to a close the three officers piled into a weapons carrier and chugged abroad while the light lasted. The island was blacked out after dark and blind driving in unfamiliar territory is not easy. The consensus was that the marine officer should do all the driving, as the others hoped to have their hands full, as it were.

All proceeded according to plan. The girls were waiting, and if they were not exactly flash-birds no one noticed. They were friendly, humorous, well-scrubbed, American, and completely enchanting. They were what Hammerstein's characters in "South Pacific" had in mind when they sang, "There is nothing like a dame!" They were naturally well aware of their "occupational specialty" at that time and place.

The party was fine. There were phonograph records, watery beer, spicy tinned things to eat, and some demure scuffling. The marine officer had commandeered a whole bottle of Australian brandy for his own use ("Semper Fi!") and was assigned the duty of winding the spring-driven record player and jockeying the disks.

This went on for a couple of hours and in due course, the brandy bottle being empty, the marine officer felt the need to withdraw. Somehow still able to walk, he ricocheted onto the sleeping porch and crashed, sitting bolt upright, on the bed.

Time passed.

Someone was shaking him.

"Gotta get the girls home, Captain. You O.K.?"

"Certainly. Absolutely. Be right with you."

The two plank-owners had fitted the back of the weapons carrier with mattresses. Space for four, if they were good friends.

The marine officer, feeling fully qualified to drive if not to walk, settled himself behind the wheel. He was not wearing his pistol, so his host thoughtfully handed him a Thompson as he fired up the engine.

It was pitch dark. He could use no illumination but the tiny red blackout lights. He had no clear idea of where he was going. But he was so drunk that the situation did not seem unreasonable. The party roared off into the night—young, happy, foolish and unconcerned.

By some incredible stroke of luck they made it. There was an "incident," but without consequence. At some point along the way a six-by-six rumbled up alongside, filled with dusky labor troops seeking a possible windfall. A spotlight searched the car. In its beam the marine officer swung the Thompson across his lap and pointed it carefully at the open window of the truck. He lifted his foot from throttle to brake, slowing to shoot. The six-by-six bellowed, accelerated ponderously and vanished. The weapons carrier continued on its uncertain but joyous way, and finally fetched up exactly on station. The marine officer, now a stretcher case, was thanked, bundled into the rolling boudoir, and driven home. Back at his host's quarters he was covered with a tarp against rain squalls and left to his own devices. The next day, curiously enough, he felt only a little the worse for wear.

Two days later in the forenoon the captain found himself bobbing out across the choppy harbor in another whale boat, headed for a dreary looking cargo ship scheduled to weigh anchor with the evening tide. As he drew near he became aware that all was not exactly in order. He had stood hundreds of deck watches on a ship-of-the-line, and what was going on aboard and close aboard this sorry sea-mule was a scandal. A dozen small craft milled around below the quarter deck, on which a thin and obviously ineffectual naval officer strove simultaneously to organize a large crowd of boarders and direct the boats into some sort of orderly approach. The marine officer perceived it to be what he had come to call a Chinese Fire Drill, such as the police today refer to as Father's-Day-in-Harlem. His deeply ingrained devotion to good order and discipline, forcefully inculcated over the years, was revolted. He set his jaw and charged headlong into the mess.

At the top of the accommodation ladder his "Request permission to come on board!" was more an order than a petition. The harassed ensign who had the deck was the only officer in sight.

"Quite a party you got here, Mister. Need a hand?"

"Well . . . I guess. Well . . . sure! What . . . ?"

"You sort out the boats. I'll see about all these people on deck. O.K.?"

There were about two hundred men, of all three services, crowded onto the main deck. In fifteen minutes the marine officer had them separated, with their gear, into three companies, with a senior non-commissioned officer in charge of each. Standing at ease in ranks, they took up a lot less room. Conversation was stilled and it was again possible to hear an order.

He returned to the grateful but confused officer of the deck.

"Where do I find the officer in charge of troops?"

"The *who?*"

"Well, the ship's secretary, or whoever will endorse my orders?"

"Uh. I, uh. I don't really know. Nobody told me we were expecting all this. Aren't *you* in charge?"

"Me? Hell, no. I'm a passenger. All by myself. I've got orders to ride this . . . ah . . . ship to San Francisco. I'm aboard. Where do I sign in?"

"I just don't know, Lieutenant," muttered the unhappy young man. "Nothing has been set up yet."

"I'm not a lieutenant—I'm a captain. And I think I'd better speak to the captain. Where is he?"

"Oh, you can't do that." The ensign seemed genuinely shocked. "Nobody sees the captain in port. He never comes out of his cabin in port."

"I see. Well, where's the executive officer?"

"Ashore. But he'll be back before we shove off." The thought cheered him up somewhat. "He's bound to be."

"Now that's real nice. Well, I guess orders can wait. Evidently they'll have to. O.K. Where's my cabin?"

"Your what?"

"My cabin, Mister, or my bunk, or whatever. You know—where I'm going to settle in for the voyage. It's a long way to Stateside, as I remember. Look, all this has been arranged!"

The deck officer backed away nervously and came up sharply against a winch. He gestured defensively with limp hands.

"Lieutenant—I mean Captain, sir—we're not a passenger ship, or even a troop ship. We carry stuff, not people. I guess the only reason you guys are coming aboard now is that all the stuff goes out—only people go back. But we can't put you anywhere but on the main deck. There's just no room!"

"Well, I'll be damned!" said the marine officer to himself, "I sure will. 'First available transportation' it says—and this is it. I wonder if anyone has thought about food. Obviously this young gentleman can't find his left hand with his right on a foggy day. The captain does not sound promising. Let's hope the exec knows his job. Let's hope. I guess we don't assign our best people to tubs like this."

Aloud. "Mister, I'll see what I can do about organizing this deck cargo of yours. When the exec comes aboard let me know immediately. Tell him—yes, tell him that I am O-in-C of troops. We have a lot to straighten out. Carry on!"

"Aye, aye, sir!" The ensign actually saluted. A good sign.

The marine officer took position on the midships hatch and directed his three deputies to have their men fall in. He summoned up his best drill-ground manner. Standing comfortably at attention, he commanded "AT EASE!" and spoke:

"Men, as a captain of marines I am the senior member of this assembly of personnel returning to the States on board this vessel. As such, I am acting officer in charge of troops, and I am now assuming command over all passengers, subject to the authority of this ship's captain, pending receipt of orders to the contrary.

"This is not a passenger ship, and it has no accommodations for us. We will make out as best we can, however, and since we're going home we can put up with a good deal for three or four weeks.

"I will do what can be done to see that our basic needs are met. I have placed a responsible man in charge of each contingent—army, navy, and marines—and he will now proceed to organize your living space in shipshape fashion.

"We will see about your papers as soon as our living conditions are taken care of.
"ATTENTION!
"Sergeants, and Chief, take charge."

All of this was very high-handed, irregular, and probably even illegal, but it worked. Everyone concerned felt that conditions were improved, and that someone was at last in charge who demonstrated both authority and responsibility. Nothing succeeds like success—especially in wartime.

As everybody knows, the backbone of any military service is to be found in its senior non-commissioned personnel. Once they had been given a sense of direction, the sergeants and petty officers fell to, dividing up the tasks, and worked wonders. Cots, hammocks, and collision mats were discovered, appropriated, and assigned. Gear was stowed and lashed down. Latrines were scrubbed, decks were swept, and trash was burned. Temporary tables of organization were prepared, according to rank and seniority, and a chain of command established.

All this was done before the exec returned aboard in the early afternoon, only a little drunk. He was a two-striper—the same grade as the marine officer—and he displayed an air of competence that was unique among the unimpressive crew.

To business at once.
"Who's in charge of passengers?" the marine officer asked.
"It seems you are."
"I have no such orders. I'm just doing what must be done until the man with the orders shows up."
"I don't think he will. We'll be underway in two hours, and I don't see any more boats approaching."
"Signal the harbormaster."
"No. He's got better things to do." The exec turned to the marine officer and grinned amiably.
"What do we need with orders?" he said. "We've got us a gyrene!"

A long pause ensued. By raising a scene, the whole business might be delayed. By insisting on propriety the book would be satisfied, but no one would gain and two hundred men who desperately wanted to see home again would wait at least a week—maybe two—maybe six. On the other hand the marine officer was straying far out of line. He was assuming authority with no right to do so. Courts martial can be very depressing.

Naturally the thought of his wife made up his mind. A court for a thing like this was not likely in a major war. Nits were not picked at that time as they have been since. The objective was more important than the format, and the objective here was clearcut. Let's get on with it!

"O. K., Lieutenant. I'm O-in-C. But I've got to be sure of a couple of things."
"Such as?"
"Food. Your boy didn't know about us. Does anyone?"

"He didn't make quarters yesterday, and nobody clued him in. We know about you. We have the chow. You'll have to furnish the messmen, though."

"We can do that. Out of two hundred we can find some cooks. What about water?"

"One gallon fresh per man per day, including cooking—unless the evaporators break down. You'll wash with sea water. We do the same."

"That will do. It will have to. Another thing."

"Yes?"

"If I'm O-in-C, I must have a free hand. All ship's orders go through me, and otherwise the whole passenger contingent is my business. No interference."

"This is the Captain's ship, as you know. He is God once we're underway. I can't do anything about that. But I don't see any problem. He is not interested in you guys."

"What sort of man is he?"

"Merchant skipper. Two-and-a-half stripes but no naval background. Old guy. A good enough navigator but a lush in port. Wish I knew where he gets the stuff."

"So you run the ship?"

"That's right. Except that he tells me where we go, and when."

"I see." The marine officer stared coldly at the exec. "What's your date of rank, Lieutenant?"

"Last April 20th. What's yours?"

"A year ago February. You can call me 'Sir'."

"Yes, Sir. But you remember who runs the ship. Sir."

"I'll remember. And we'll get along just fine."

And they did. Mainly by staying well out of each other's way.

The cattle boat, as they came to call it, chugged its way northeastward, alone on the bright blue sea. The war was not yet won but any prowling Nip submarines or patrol craft would be unlikely to betray their location by attacking an insignificant cargo ship on its way out of the combat zone. In any case no destroyer nor corvette could be spared for escort duty. That was a war we intended to win, and the watchword was "Attack!" Let defense take care of itself.

The marine officer found out just before departure that he was not the senior passenger, as he had thought. Two army doctors, both majors, slipped aboard just as the ship was getting underway, and their rank took precedence. They had not, however, the slightest interest in giving any orders. With proper military punctilio they were assigned the choicest piece of deck as their "quarters" and were respectfully saluted whenever anyone noticed them. The marine officer continued in what might be termed "kangaroo command."

After various tarps, shields, and awnings were rigged, life on an exposed deck in the tropical Pacific became quite comfortable. That can be a balmy and pleasant ocean—in its good moods—and it was on its good behavior on the run up to Hawaii, stopping only at Christmas Island. The food was—well—food. It was not good but it sufficed.

The marine officer instituted a routine of cleanliness and "busy work" to balk the devil, who, as we know, always finds work for idle hands. The troops grumbled a bit at this but that was a good sign. When troops *don't* grumble it is time to watch out.

An office of sorts was set up and everybody's orders were processed, establishing that each man had indeed been aboard the vessel for the stipulated period so that leave time could be calculated from the expected date of debarkation. The marine officer signed all papers, including those of the two doctors, but did nothing at all about his own. He considered the matter and concluded that whoever eventually scanned his orders would have less to rule on if nothing confusing was set down in print. His orders directed him to report, after thirty days leave en route, to the commanding general at Camp Pendleton. So he would do exactly that. If his endorsements were incomplete so be it. He had done as he was bid, and if he did various irregular things along the way he could claim that he was commissioned by the President of the United States to exercise initiative—among other things.

Day followed day, alternating with brilliant, starlit nights. Going home!

> *"Kiss me once*
> *And kiss me twice,*
> *And kiss me once again.*
> *It's been a long, long time!"*

"Yes, God, it's been *years!*" Soldiers have felt this way since the world was virginal, ". . . and the young sun shone like fire on the red metal of their new and greedy swords."

The ship plowed on. How many days now? Twenty? Twenty-five? With any kind of luck it won't be thirty. Lord, lord, lord!

One carries his world within himself, and where he is is the world. Elsewhere is acknowledged, but it cannot be accepted as real, because reality is here and now. Other places have the substance of fiction. The marine officer knew that there was such a place as California—he had grown up there—but after two-and-a-half years of war it had no more reality for him than Tudor England or the Africa of the Great Trek.

But now, barring disaster, he really would know it again. He could not dream, for the thought of his wife's slim, graceful, dancer's body drove him to madness.

He invented work to do. Gun drill. Abandon ship drill. Fire drill. Air bedding. Swab decks. Calisthenics. Keep busy!

There came a day when the ship dropped the hook in Pearl Harbor. No liberty was granted. The men resented this vocally, but it was sound policy. They were going home, and there was no need for any expensive and possibly damaging debauch on the way.

The last leg became cold and unpleasant on the open deck. The Pacific off San Francisco can be raw and nasty. The passengers during those last few days sought shivering shelter from the cold salt spray, but they did not complain. Soon, now! They had survived, and they could look forward to living again.

"War's begun in '41
Prove you're true in '42
Over the sea in '43
Win the war in '44
Stay alive in '45
The world to fix in '46
Closer to Heaven in '47
    GOLDEN GATE IN '48"

Well, it was only '44, *and there was the Golden Gate!*
The marine officer, in his formal green uniform and tailored bridge coat, stood by his packed gear in the flying spray at the ship's waist as she slid under the bridge into the bay. Having assumed a command that had never been assigned to him, he was perfectly willing to relinquish it without ceremony. All passengers were neat, clean, and healthy. They were also in San Francisco Bay. It seemed enough.

Two patrol boats escorted the ship. As one closed to within earshot he made a mischievous decision. He sprang up on the rail, megaphone in hand, and shouted, "Twenty-two! Lay alongside!"

As the boat obediently approached he issued quick orders to a couple of NCO's. The craft touched gently and his baggage was quickly dropped overside into the tender.

He asked no permission. He said no goodbyes. He snapped a quick "Well done!" to his deputies, came to attention, saluted aft, and dropped down the fixed rungs into the boat.

"Sheer off, Cox'n!" And he was gone. He felt a pang about deserting all those people he had tended throughout the long voyage, but it passed. "They're home," he thought. "They're O.K. The paper pushers can take charge. And I will now take charge of myself."

He spoke to the coxswain, a boatswain's mate second-class.

"What are your orders?"

"Pick up the mail, sir. Take off emergency personnel. Deliver, and return to base."

"Very well. You can drop me anywhere on the Embarcadero, and carry on."

"Aye aye, sir. Pier Seven O.K.?"

"Pier Seven will do nicely, thank you."

The San Francisco waterfront was quite operational, despite the times. The boat crew even helped him find a taxi. Somehow he didn't think there would be any taxis, but he was happy enough to make use of one.

First he got his trunk and foot locker to a freight office, and consigned them to his home address. Then he was driven down the old Bayshore Highway to the airport. The taxi driver was friendly, but his attitude seemed strange. His conversation was guarded and he displayed no interest in the far thunder in the Pacific.

Returning soldiers are invariably surprised, and a bit wistful, to find that nobody on the home front has any interest in what they have been doing. The home front is a troubled and unhappy place, and its denizens don't really understand what's going on.

"Come all you Virginia gals
Fix your hair with pins
Give them wine and kisses, but
DON'T ASK THEM WHERE THEY'VE BEEN."

They may wonder why not. Where they have been is what they now are, and to them it's pretty interesting. It does not seem so, however, to the people back home.

The marine officer gave it no thought. His mind was on other things.

Passage to Burbank in a DC-3 was easily arranged. Air travel was much simpler then. Within an hour the marine officer was airborne, winging his way down California's central valley. He had called ahead, and the response at the other end had been understandably dramatic.

At the Burbank Airport he took the downtown bus. There being no freeways, the bus route took him right down Rossmore Avenue, and his father's house was Number 500 North.

The sun had set as he crossed the street, a suitcase in each hand. This was the street of his youth. His world had come back to center. The house in which he had grown up looked exactly the same. It was unbelievable, and yet at the same time very natural.

There were three blood-red stars displayed in the front window. His mother's two sons and son-in-law were away at war. She was at the door. His wife was not to be seen.

Embraced, his mother said, "She's upstairs. In your room."

His soul on fire, he took the stairs three at a time, raced down the hall . . .

And then she was naked in his arms.

A man cannot faint dead away from pure joy, but if he could have he would have.

6

To An American Serving in Viet Nam

*A*T THE COMING OF ANOTHER CHRISTMAS, *we of Bear Valley extend to you our warmest and most affectionate greetings. Far as you are from the scenes you remember as home, you may know that those you left there are constant in their pride, admiration, and gratitude for what you are and what you are doing. Do not be misled by that irresponsible and misguided fraction of our people whose shrill cries are given inordinate attention by many who should know better—rather be assured that the great majority of the decent people of your country are fully aware of your defense of our vital interests and regard your skill, courage, and moral hardihood with reverent awe.*

This is a time of confusion, in which principles and policies are often in apparent conflict. But this is no new thing—soldiers have known it since the days of the Pharaohs. Though you may well wonder at the seemingly pointless, yet still deadly, demands of a war you are not permitted to win, please remember that we know you speedily could win it if you were so directed. The soldier's pride must always remain rooted in himself and his organization, taking little account of international complexities which he is seldom in a position to study. In any case we at home know, as well as you do, that this most unsatisfactory war has the best and clearest moral justification of any this country has ever fought. You fight now to contain the march of world tyranny, to make the world enemy know that he may not force the subjugation of people who reject his odious philosophy, to establish that murder must not become an acceptable political tactic, and to let the world know that the United States of America keeps its word. These are good reasons—perhaps the best we ever had!

It's not fun out where you are, as most of your fathers know from personal experience, but perhaps it is some comfort to know that, while you face the storm on the wall, those whom you protect, warm and safe in the rear, know that they can remain so only because of you. We hope that this small gift we send you will symbolize that knowledge. It's not much, but the spirit behind it is most sincere.

God bless you all, and Merry Christmas!

7

Home
of the
Brave

ONE OF THE MOST MEMORABLE SECTIONS of Tom Lea's memorable novel, *The Brave Bulls*, deals with the visit of the impressario, Eladio Gomez, to a mythical bull ranch known as Las Astas, where the Homeric figure of Don Tiburcio Balbuena raises the finest fighting bulls in all Mexico.

By a fortunate chance I was once able to pay a similar visit to the reality on which Las Astas was based, and I found reality to be fully as fascinating as fancy.

In the extreme northeast corner of Jalisco, some 25 miles east of the city of Aguascalientes, lie the holdings of the Madrazo family, 125,000 acres, *mas o menos*, comprising the two ranches of La Punta and Matancillas, a hundred-year-old estate where the blue blood of the primeval aurochs is maintained with the devoted care of a vestal flame.

In a world increasingly inclined to compromise, "make-do," and cost-accounting, it is a joy to encounter an enterprise based on quality alone, with *no* short-cuts, just-as-goods, or forced economies. La Punta raises bulls, fighting bulls, *toros de lidia*, and *one* bourgeois specimen among a whole season's output of aristocrats is a disaster. Necessarily, La Punta is dedicated to perfection.

For a fighting bull is no accident. He is not a natural phenomenon. He is not a wild creature which will fight for his life if threatened. He is not a predator which kills to eat. He is not even (usually) a herd sire defending his family rights. He is an artificially bred engine of death. This is a principal point which is not understood by the detractors of the Fiesta. The bull is a creature totally outside their experience, since he is only to be found at bullfights and on bull ranches. As the symbol, incarnation, and eager agent of death—created not by nature but by man—the fighting bull is simply not comparable to any other living creature.

These animals are raised on a few ranches in Spain and Mexico. They have never been domesticated, in the sense that beef or dairy cattle have. But even this fact does not account for their nature, since a totally wild animal will lose its wildness in an environment which contains no enemies. On the bull ranches, to the contrary, the original savagery of ancient sires is cultivated like the milk production of a dairy cow, until the end product is fit to represent Death himself in the ring.

I arrived at La Punta early one morning in July. The second month of the rains had turned the high prairie a dozen shades of green, and the cleanly washed air moved enough to feel distinctly chilly. A simple, two-word, road sign marked the turnoff and the paved driveway led through pleasantly spaced mesquite and nopal toward the foot of a line of high, rocky bluffs to the northeast. At the first cattle guard I reached the region in which it is better to stay in one's car, and almost at once the jet-black, glossy forms appeared. Never in groups, but widely spaced individuals and pairs, these were the young bulls passing their adolescence between their first testing and their selection for stud or the ring. Even at first glance they bore no resemblance to tame cattle. They moved more like leopards than oxen.

Less than five miles from the highway I found the hacienda, first apparent from the old adobe walls of the original buildings which date from the time of Benito Juárez. The "new house," built in 1907, is set back within a large grove of pepper trees adjoining the earlier construction, and the grounds are exotically decorated with flocks of peacocks.

The sun was slanting over the bluffs and several charros were standing around in the dawn chill, puffing on home-rolled cigarillos and waiting for the day's chores to be assigned. I asked for the dueño and was directed to the foreyard of the new house where two men were standing. They were both Madrazos, owners and operators of La Punta and Matancillas, and direct descendants of the Spaniard, Don Ignacio Madrazo, who was granted title to the present estates—two parcels of 25,000 hectares apiece—in 1864.

That year all correspondence listed two brothers, José and Francisco, as the operators of La Punta. As it happens, both were semi-retired and operations were managed almost entirely by young Don Francisco, the son of Francisco the elder. Since Don José is a bachelor, the younger man was not only acting manager but sole heir to this regal fief, and it was he and his uncle who greeted me.

Both wore boots, spurs and gloves, but while Don José wore a linen jacket and a curious, down-turned sombrero, young Don Francisco wore a leather jacket and the stiff-brimmed, flat-crowned, felt hat of Andalucía.

Don José replied to my request for a look at his noble animals with grave courtesy, indicating that "the boy" was just going out to supervise feeding and that I might go along. "The boy" was Don Francisco, a suggestion of the patriarchal attitude of the hidalgo.

We set out in a pickup truck, loaded with bags of grain, and accompanied by one grizzled charro who could have served as a model for a postcard.

As this was high summer, the bulls for the winter season had already been selected, assigned to corridas, purchased, and confined to 250-hectare "potreros" so that they could become accustomed to each other and fill out their already formidable frames on a grain diet. Individual stone basins were situated some distance apart to avoid cause for argument. Placidity in a fighting bull is always the most fragile of moods, and two would only need an instant to cost La Punta several thousand dollars.

We drove near the basins and two ranch hands broke open bags of corn and filled the hollow stones. The charro set up a piercing whistling and presently black forms came quietly from among the trees. Coming in a group, heads down, they looked a bit like ordinary cattle. One could make a mistake, but not many.

"These are one *corrida*," said Francisco. "They are already chosen for the Plaza at Morelia. They will fight in the fall. Meanwhile they grow strong on grain."

As they moved up to the bins they spaced out, and two asserted their unwillingness to be pressured by squaring off rather formally with their horns.

"Will they attack a car?" I asked.

"Sometimes," answered Francisco, "but probably not this car. They are used to it."

I noted the variety of horn configuration, and remarked to Francisco about one bull whose points curved inward toward each other. He mentioned that the toreros, with good reason, liked this kind. Another, which I photographed, had widespread, outward-directed points.

"He is more dangerous," I ventured.

"*Todos son peligrosos*"—"They are *all* dangerous." It was clear that this was a point of honor with Francisco.

This was established at once. In a familiar group the young bulls do not rouse quickly, but when isolated even for a moment the carefully nurtured fury springs forth like the jaws of a trap. One had strayed and the charro had found him. It was quite a sight.

As we approached we could see bull and horseman facing each other. The veteran charro kept the bulk of a massive nopal between them with superb horsemanship, but the bull was striving for a clear shot at him. The jet-black, 800-pound animal acted like nothing so much as a terrier waiting for the ball to be thrown. Head up, hooves forward, he darted on spring-steel muscles, moving quickly from one "launching pad" to the next. With each move the charro countered, sidling behind the cactus thickets and continually shrilling "chow call" from experienced lips. Finally, bored and irritated with this target he couldn't fix, the bull whirled like a cat and bounded away toward the feeding bins.

"This is a careful business," I said.

"Yes," said Francisco, "one is careful or one does not succeed."

This portion of the huge ranch is divided into a generous number of potreros. There are many plazas in Mexico and La Punta must be prepared, four-and-a-half years in advance, to furnish any or all of them with one or more corridas each season. At the time of my visit, eleven potreros were occupied with selected corridas, each of which included one or more spares to take care of accidents in transit or any discoverable flaw between ranch and toril. The plaza assumes all reponsibility for the bulls f.o.b., but the risk is traditionally met in this fashion, which is in the interest of the rancher's reputation as well as that of the impressario. Each corrida is purchased for a fixed sum, including spares. Since the bigger plazas pay more for the best stock, the unit price of a fighting bull varies, but La Punta averaged 10,000 pesos ($800) at that time—perhaps ten times that sum now.

As we moved from one potrero to another, Francisco told me how the quality of his stock is maintained. The calves are separated from the cows (a delicate operation) at eight months, branded with an individual number and recorded by pedigree. At one year bull calves are tested in the ring, with pic only. Shown an unfamiliar horseman, they charge, to be met with the regulation iron-tipped lance of the picador. The coarse point drives two inches or more into the shoulder, but the little bull must hurl himself against it again and again, trying only to close in and kill. If he does not—veal. There is always plenty of fresh meat on a bull ranch.

The standard is valor, not percentage. If all the calves meet the test, fine—a good year. If none does—*es lástima*—but all are slaughtered. La Punta bulls *must* come through. Over the years about 50% qualify for the ring.

The bulls are not tested again, and are never shown a cape or muleta, unless they are selected for stud. The ranch maintains about 16 studs, and whenever one outlives his usefulness another must be selected. From the very best arena-bound four-year-olds, a few with the finest pedigrees, color, size, configuration, and horn are chosen. These are brought to the ring and tested again, this time with everything—cape, pic, and muleta. They are brought right up to the death by Mexico's finest matadors, performing in private, and again about half pass the test. These are reprieved from death in the ring and granted a life of bovine bliss, marred only by the absence of the ecstasy of destruction which is their reason for being. To grow old and die without blood on his horns is an ignominy, in a way, for a brave bull.

The cows they mount are in every way the equal of the bulls in spirit, ferocity, and valor. Heifers are recorded as carefully as bull calves, and tested fully at the age of 3½. Here the attrition is even greater than with the bulls. About one in four shows the quality to bear a La Punta bull, the rest are beef.

In this fashion, over the years, the absolute cream of the original Andalusian Barladé blood line is maintained—each generation carrying on the finest fraction of its predecessor's "casta." This sort of breeding is not unusual in other strains of pedigreed animals, but usually it is conducted with an eye to configuration only, or the record of meat, milk or egg production. With the bulls it is 90% spirit and only 10% form.

After the morning feeding we returned past the intricately designed structure that is used for testing, sorting and crating. It is based on a standard size bull ring (without, of course, the grandstand) surrounded by a system of enclosures and runways through which individual animals may be moved without touching them. One thing about bull ranching is simpler than with tame cattle. You don't have to herd your stock—just attract attention and it comes to you—quickly!

In one of the pens we found a middle aged seed bull, brought in for examination. Standing on the runway just inside the parapet, I slapped the wall with my hand. Instantly the black form spun around and froze. Then the heavy, goring muscles of the neck crested, the bright black stare focused, and with a slight up-and-down motion of the polished horns, he zeroed in on the intruder and waited.

Next to me, Francisco murmured, *"¡Es listo!"* "He's ready!"

It's a curious sensation to confront a creature that wants you dead, just because you are alive. The bull could not eat me and I was no threat to him, from his experience, but he wanted to kill me because, like Mallory's Everest, "I was there." Of all living creatures this is the only one which is large and strong enough to kill a man, is wholly inimical to man, and has not the slightest fear of man.

He did not paw the ground or bellow. This is threat, and the blooded toro de lidia does not threaten. He fears it might frighten you into flight, and he doesn't want you to flee. The great, black chest heaved and he whuffed through his nostrils. The black eyes blazed a message, "Don't run, don't leave. Come down off that wall. See, I stand perfectly still. Just come down off that wall!"

"A great animal," I said. "A señor toro!"

"Yes," said Francisco. "He is ten years old and he has the same spirit he had at three. A fine sire!"

We returned to the house and sat down to breakfast in the great dining room beneath high oak rafters and surrounded by pictures of noble bulls and famous matadors that have contributed to the tradition of La Punta. Breakfast was, naturally, "huevos rancheros"—eggs fried straight up in green chile salsa and served on a tortilla with a side order of refritos.

I congratulated Francisco on what appeared to me to be a magnificent life—I had never encountered such an impressive combination of a vigorous outdoor existence, an established and honored place in the life of his country, a noble tradition to maintain and improve, and about as much financial security as is possible in an uncertain world. He agreed, modestly, that it was a good life; especially when his wife and child were present at the hacienda, which was most of the year.

I asked him what his principal problems were—since everyone has some—and he said there was only one—the critics.

"We do absolutely the best we know how. We leave nothing to chance. Our standards are all but unachievable. And in nine hundred and ninety-nine cases we succeed. Then comes the thousandth case—a bad La Punta bull—and the sky falls in! The critics call it everything from betrayal of a sacred trust to a deliberate attempt to sabotage the Fiesta. They are right, of course, in claiming that the public has the right to expect good bulls from La Punta, but one might be reasonable."

"That's the curse of excellence," I reflected. "The mediocre don't have that problem. I don't believe you'd want to trade with them, would you?"

"No," said Francisco, with a smile, "I prefer it this way."

As I drove back to the highway I wondered what reaction I would get from an article on this impressive hacienda. The whole idea of the bullfight is regarded as repellent by some, and if their ideas on the subject are frozen, they cannot approve of the breeding of fighting bulls. However, for those whose minds are open, even if they have no appreciation or understanding of the bull festival, I would like to raise two points. First, the fighting bull would not exist at all if it were not for the corrida. The descendants of the aurochs would either be extinct or bred down to an unrecognizable meat-producing machine. Second, which life is preferable: That of a dull-witted, lumbering, sexless oaf, doomed to spiritless slavery and an ignoble, defenseless death; or that of an active, heads-up, undaunted, virile warrior, dying in hot blood at the very peak of strength and vigor? Personally, I don't think there's much of a choice.

8

Inferno on Foot

NATURALISTS AND TRAVEL WRITERS never tire of saying that one cannot appreciate the Grand Canyon of the Colorado from its rims. They usually suggest mule rides down a bit into the depths. But muleback is a rather meek and dispirited way to travel, and in our family we have an aversion to impersonating dead freight, so we decided that we could go anyplace a mule could, and crossed the Canyon on foot.

Our efforts were well worth the trouble, for now we can say that we have, in a sense, walked "to hell and back" and we enjoyed every step of the way. This is not to say that the Canyon's bottom is unpleasant, for Phantom Ranch is a charming oasis, but the depths of the inner gorge are definitely Satanic in aspect, and penetrating them on one's own two feet, without being carried by vehicle or beast of burden, is an experience that borders upon the occult.

The canyon walk is not a wilderness adventure. One is confined to trails by park regulation and there is little sense of the wild, but this awesome gorge is the cathedral of the earth, and intimacy with it produces a perspective toward creation and man's place in it that may be a beginning of wisdom.

Statistics often glance off the mind like hail off a steep roof, and the specifications of the Canyon are astronomically beyond comprehension, so I won't quote many

FireWorks

of them here. But basically the journey to the bottom starts 200,000,000 years ago at the surface (for erosion has planed the Kaibab plateau down through the Mesozoic Era) and penetrates down into the unthinkable, lifeless youth of the world, one and a half billion years ago.

We decided to walk from North Rim to South, as the North Rim is both higher above and farther from the river. Sleeping accommodations were secured at Phantom Ranch, in the bottom, and we carried two lunches, a breakfast, and a dinner in our packs. Since the trip is only about 25 miles, it *could* be made in a single day, but our aim was to soak up the experience, not just to cover the ground, so we allowed most of two days. To give us proper understanding of the experience, we persuaded Dr. J.G. Marks, whose Ph.D. is in geology, to accompany us. This made the trip a success.

Mid-June is about as early as the hike may be attempted, as the North Rim facilities are snowed shut until late spring. By this time it's already warm down at the river, a mile below, and as the summer progresses it grows hot. Crossing the Canyon in midwinter would be an interesting experience, but special arrangements have to be made with the U.S. Park Service.

We started down the Kaibab Trail at 8 A.M., following a veritable boulevard of a footpath which could very nearly accommodate a jeep. The North Rim, at some 8,500 feet, is well up into the Canadian life zone, where the Stellar Jay squawks from the glimmering aspen. It was cool and fresh as we cut down through the Kaibab stratum toward the first great layer, the Coconino Sandstone. This enormous wall, 300 feet of vertical beige rock, is startlingly evident on both sides of the Canyon. It was deposited through scores of millions of years of the Permian period by windblown sand. Its pale, even surface forms the topmost towers of the major buttes of the Canyon. In evidence of the unearthly calm of this ancient age, we found rocks on which pre-dinosaurian reptiles had run between fossil raindrops. It's hard to imagine a world in which a spate of light rain was the only prominent phenomenon occurring for decades, enabling individual droplets to be frozen forever into a sand dune.

Below the Coconino wall we found the Supai layers of softer red rocks, and we entered the transition life zone. The Supai layer crumbles away at a 45-degree slope for several hundred feet to the top of the Redwall, and takes us down nearly to 300,000,000 years. Those who think that Shakespeare, living 300 years ago, was pretty ancient, may gulp to realize that, as they stand on the Redwall, their feet tread rock *one million times* as old as Elizabethan England.

The Kaibab Trail (North) runs down Roaring Springs Canyon to its junction with Bright Angel Canyon, and thence some ten miles due south to the Colorado River. At the mouth of Roaring Springs Canyon pure, fresh water gushes out of the base of the Redwall and forms Roaring Springs, the noise of which, due to the uncanny acoustics of the Canyon, can be distinctly heard at Bright Angel Point, 3,800 feet above. (This is more than 3½ Empire State Buildings, if you're fond of comparisons.)

The Redwall, of Mississippian limestone, is the second "grand tier" of the Canyon. Interestingly enough it is red only to the depth of a coat of paint, its basic grey color having been washed over by iron-red seepage from the Supai layer above. Coming down through it, the trail is in some places grooved out of the solid rock, and travel is distinctly "airy." At this point I for one was glad to be on my own feet, and not those of some mule I had never met before and with whom I had probably nothing in common.

At Roaring Springs we stopped for lunch. Travelling slowly, with frequent pauses to admire both the scenery and the stratigraphy, we used up half a day on this first leg. There is no water between the rim and the Springs, but since it is all downhill none is needed. The reverse route, from Roaring Springs up to the rim, could be a bit harsh for anyone out of condition.

The Springs are in the lower transition life zone, and to my surprise I found them frequented by that curious sierran bird, the water ouzel, who flies under water. We found ouzels the full length of Bright Angel Creek, certainly an odd habitat for a bird of the snow country.

Below the Springs, the gradient is very gentle for the full length of the tributary canyon. The life zone is primarily Sonoran until the black rocks of the inner gorge are reached, where it becomes, unscientifically but descriptively, "Infernian."

We passed the power house, whence electricity generated by Bright Angel Creek is fed to the rim high above, and plunged on down through Cambrian strata into the heat.

For it did get hot. In spite of the rollicking crystal stream always within earshot, we began to feel distinctly like Palm-Springs-in-the-Summer. However, a couple of deep green pools, plus the spectacular red-green-and-silver Ribbon Falls, gave us the opportunity to rinse away both dust and sweat.

Down and down and down. Mile on mile on mile. At the bottom of the Cambrian strata we were 500,000,000 years back toward the birth of the world—five hundred times the age of the first proto-human, and beyond even the incredible ages of the time of fishes, whose strata are curiously absent from the walls of the Grand Canyon.

And now Bright Angel Canyon narrowed and closed around us, as we cut through the Tapeat Sandstone and down into the fearful, archean bowels of the earth. The shadows close in. The rock is black and gleams with mica. Strata are crushed and shattered and blasted with granitic veins of billion-year-old-magma. It is so hot that you cannot touch a rock that has been hours in the shade. The canyon walls are vertical. Here is Dante's Inferno. At any sudden turn you could meet Lucifer himself glowering upon his black throne. If you have any imagination at all you will never forget this.

The inner gorge is *one and one half billion years old,* far antedating any vestige of life on this planet.

Finally, passing the eerie mouth of the slit that is Phantom Canyon, there was a gleam of cottonwoods and we arrived at Phantom Ranch. Here are air-cooled cabins, a cool emerald pool, and iced beer. An outpost of the human race in the Devil's realm. When we retired at 9 P.M. on an early June evening, it was 101 degrees F.; but the evaporators kept the cabins cool enough to require at least a sheet.

A dim, dawn start saw us off down the ¾ mile to the river. The deer herd was so tame we almost had to shoulder our way through it. At the bottom, near where the clear waters of Bright Angel join the muddy torrent, is the Kaibab suspension bridge. This structure, built in 1928, is astonishing when one recalls that it had to be constructed entirely without the help of wheeled or tracked vehicles. The suspension cables for its 350-foot length had to be snaked down the trail on the backs of porters.

On the south bank the trail proceeds a few hundred yards and then forks. The left (East) fork is the Kaibab Trail (South). It is steep and waterless and reaches the South Rim at Yaki Point. On foot, *it should only be used for the descent.* The right hand (West) fork, some four miles longer, is the Bright Angel Trail. In addition to an intermittent flow at the mouth of Pipe Canyon, this trail touches three water points. It is the sensible way up.

For two miles, Bright Angel Trail follows the banks of the mighty river, carved out of the azoic black walls of the inner gorge. Then it suddenly vanishes into a narrow black cleft in the south wall—Pipe Canyon.

In the dim light of early day the walking was pleasant and the hellish aspect of the canyon bottom was mitigated by the lack of the preceding day's fierce heat, but long banners of light striking horizontally among the tremendous towers above us indicated that it would not remain cool for long.

Up Pipe Canyon for two miles we kept to a gentle gradient, and then, in a sudden series of zigzags, the trail leapt up the west wall—right up out of the "hellrocks" and into the Cambrian stratum. Here again we walked in a region that had known life.

As we slanted up through the Tapeat Sandstone toward the Tonto Platform we began dodging from one bit of shade to the next, for the morning sun was already hot, and, unlike the previous day's walk, this was all uphill. At 9 A.M. we pulled into Indian Gardens, the cottonwood oasis so visible from the lodges on the South Rim, and paused for brunch.

There is plenty of water and shade at Indian Gardens, 4½ miles below the rim, and here, if it were possible, the trip should end. Most mule visitors go down only as far as Roaring Springs on the North or Indian Gardens on the South. The North Rim—Roaring Springs trail is not heavily travelled, it was downhill for us, and between Roaring Springs and Indian Gardens we had the Canyon almost to ourselves. However, the leg from Indian Gardens to the South Rim is steep, hot, dusty, and so heavily mule-travelled that it resembles a trail through a stable. It is almost due North-South so one cannot avoid the sun. There is practically no shade. There are two water points above Indian Gardens, so one does not suffer from thirst. But the heat, the dust, and the reek make it an unpleasant climb—a price that must be paid for the rest of the trip.

Doing it again, I would consult the calendar and arrange to come up by the light of a full moon. In addition to avoiding both heat and mules, this would add an additional sense of the weird to an already surrealistic adventure. One could leave Phantom Ranch at 10 P.M. and comfortably reach the rim by dawn.

The Canyon crossing, about 25 miles in all, is not for the aged and infirm, nor for the very young. It is not for the heat sensitive nor for those with tender feet. But few things of value in this world are available just for the asking. Those who are prepared to face a little heat or cold, a little thirst or weariness, will live a richer life for it.

The Grand Canyon is one of the mighty sights of the world. It is close to us, but far for those who will not seek its heart. For those who will, it can provide expansion of soul achievable in no other way.

9

Venison Harvest

MUCH HAS BEEN WRITTEN about the technique of deer hunting, and much of it has been good. The greater part has been devoted to the problem of finding deer, which is certainly understandable since not much can be done with a deer you haven't found. Still, the subject of what to do from the point of contact forward has not been so well covered, though the hunter's actions at this time can radically affect the outcome of the entire enterprise.

I am a mediocre deer hunter. Among other things I lack sufficient patience. So I am content to sit at the feet of those never-failing masters of the craft (who fill out their tags every year on opening day) trying to learn how to think like a buck—so far without conspicuous success. On the other hand, I am an efficient harvester of such deer as I do run across. Twice in my life I have failed to bring in an animal that I had decided to take, and my hunting mileage is long. What follows, therefore, is a guide for the novice concerning his behavior once he has arrived at his moment of truth.

Very well. You have found your quarry. After months of planning, stacks of paperwork, a good deal of travel, several hundred practice rounds, a perfectly adjusted zero, and enough hiking to satisfy a boy scout (to say nothing of enough money spent to trouble you for the rest of the year), you are looking right at a shootable buck, within range. In the next few seconds your hunt will be either a success or a failure. Pretty exciting!

So cool it! *Don't* get excited. You're a man, not a monkey. *Control yourself.* The tendency to flip your lid at this point is well nigh irresistible. Resist it. This is the test. Pass it!

You need a perfect squeeze—a surprise break. You need a solid position. You may have ten or fifteen seconds, sometimes more but often less. You must do everything right, and excuses are not acceptable.

So, first, turn off your nerves. As Hemingway put it, "freeze yourself into that impersonal state you shoot from." Psych yourself in. Think, "It's just a target . . . just a target . . . just a target." You *know* you can hit a target smaller than that. You've done it a hundred times, with the rifle you're holding now. And this is just another target. Easy does it.

Get into the steadiest position you can. Never shoot from off-hand if you can help it. If you have had any warning that a shot was coming up, you already have the sling loop on your arm. If not, looping up takes five seconds. And, from any position offering elbow support, it will raise your kill probability about 35%.

Under normal conditions you can forget trajectory. Assuming that you're using a rifle of reasonably high velocity, and that you're not trying something stupid at over 300 yards, your bullet will strike closer to the line of sight than you can hold, under field conditions. Put the cross right on the kill point and make that break a surprise.

The point you select to shoot at is crucial. As Whelen taught us, your "surgical skill as a killer" is probably more important than either your rifle or your marksmanship. Visualize your quarry as a three-dimensional mass with its vital zone located well forward and slightly below center in the body cavity. Shoot for the center of that vital zone, regardless of the relative position of the animal. Never shoot at the whole beast. Pick out the kill point and hit that.

Now—*squeeze!* Press quickly, but steadily. *Make that break a surprise.* Careful . . . careful . . . it's just a target . . . careful . . .WHAM!

(Snick the action instantly. Stay on target.)

O.K! He's down. He bucked hard, spun around, and crashed into the shrubbery. You can't see him, but he's down. *Now,* you can get excited. I don't suggest that you leap on your horse and ride madly off in all directions, like the man in the story, but you can exult. You did everything right, and you have won. Don't let anyone put your victory down. A prime buck is no easy mark. He doesn't have a rifle and he doesn't have your brains, but he is *much* better able to avoid you in the woods than you are to find him. He is much stronger, much faster, much quieter than you are. He can't see quite as well as you, but his senses of smell and hearing are completely out of your class. If he didn't just blunder on to you while involved in another problem, you have pulled off quite a feat.

Do not run forward at this point. The wound may not have been instantly fatal, and a beast who knows he is being pursued has unbelievable physical resources. I recall a bull elk that ran about 75 yards after a fatal hit and then stopped in a thicket. If we had run after him he might have gone a mile. As it was he bled out and fell where he stopped—after ten minutes.

So sit still. If you have a pre-arranged kill call to bring your partner, sound it. Pick up your empty case—it makes a nice keepsake. Note your surroundings carefully. Where is camp? Where is the nearest jeep track? What is the best route by which to retrieve the carcass? Above all, savor the moment. This is what you worked for. Parkinson's famed epigram tells us that happiness is the by-product of accomplishment. You have accomplished your mission. Life is measured by the number of big moments it includes. This is one. Appreciate it.

Unless you can see the quarry from where you are, wait fifteen minutes. This is hard, but stick it out. It may be very important. Then to work. You've got to find him now, and this is not always easy. An intervening canyon filled with brush can make it very hard to recognize the ground on the far side once you have scrambled through it. Mark your firing point. Hang your hat, or a bandana, or something brightly conspicuous, right where you shot. Then look along your line of sight to where you hit and pick out a tree or rock or bush exactly on that line, some distance out but with no intervening obstacles. Move out and mark this point with blaze tape. (You always carry ten feet of blaze tape in your pocket.) Now you have established an azimuth that will lead you right to your target. Make sure you mark it well enough so that you can see it from the other end. If there is one, note a landmark near the point where the buck fell and home on that. As you approach, pace the distance if ground permits. It is well to know how long a shot you made.

If you are hunting with a partner (usually a good idea) it is well for you to stay right at the firing point and have him make the approach. This way you need never lose sight of the hit point. When he arrives there you can guide him to that exact point by means of pre-arranged arm signals. If he can see the animal from there all is well. If not, you can join him and the two of you can commence quartering together. If you did everything right, as we have assumed up to now, your buck will be lying a few yards from where he was hit. These precautions for locating him are suggested for use in thick brush, where it is quite possible to stand within a stone's throw of a downed animal and still lose him.

There he is, the object of the enterprise! He is worthy of all your skill. Treat him with respect. You may have a trophy, and, since you killed clean with one shot, you also have probably more than your own weight of the tastiest protein in the world. At current rates that would be worth a fortune at the supermarket, if you could buy it there, and you can't. It is now your job to make sure that this superb meat winds up perfectly prepared at your household, not spoiled by bad handling.

First, the photos. The animal as he fell, alone. A close-up of his head, if he is a trophy buck. Then one with the rifle, and, if you have a partner, one with you and your rifle (action open, of course). If time permits, go back to the firing point and get a photo of yourself in position as you shot. This can be a good study and is often overlooked.

Next, get your tag on his antler.

Now clean him. Now, not later. This must never be omitted . . . not in a snowstorm . . . not because it's dark . . . not because you're pooped, or because you don't want to get bloody. Never.

Work him around so that he is on his back, head uphill. If there are other hunters around, throw your coat over his antlers. Roll up your sleeves and put your wristwatch in your shirt pocket.

Start your cut right at the wishbone. Work very carefully downward, making surgically sure that you do not cut anything but the body wall, to the anus, which you remove with a circular cut to avoid nicking the colon. A smallish knife with a blunt point but a very sharp edge is best for this. Ease the viscera out, taking care not to puncture the stomach, the intestines, or the bladder. It is imperative not to contaminate the venison by contact with any waste matter. (Slaughter houses are not always as careful as you must be. That is one reason why venison is better than commercial beef.) Locate the esophagus (the forward end of the alimentary tract), follow it well up into the neck, and cut it off. With both ends free, the entire digestive apparatus may now be removed without breaking it. Get it well clear of the carcass. Place the liver and kidneys in your string bag (you always carry a string bag, such as oranges are often sold in, for this purpose). Also the heart, if it has not been too badly torn up by your shot. These delicacies go right with you. They are best as fresh as possible. Wipe out the body cavity with a bunch of grass, and your first step is complete.

If you have a trophy buck, you may now proceed to prepare him, though if night has fallen this can wait until you get him to camp. To take a head, start with a circular cut well back behind where the neck joins the body, deep enough to free the skin. From this cut, on top of the neck but just to one side of the dorsal ridge, lead another cut forward to a point just back of the antler roots. Fork it here, and lead a short cut out to the root of each antler. Starting where the dorsal cut joins the circular cut, carefully skin out the neck. When you have worked all the skin off the neck, sever the spine from the skull and remove the head. The head and antlers, with the cape (neck skin) attached, may then be carried back to camp for complete skinning.

If your buck is not trophy material, or if you just want an antler mount without the head, it is best to get the whole carcass back to camp before working on the head.

Now you've got to get him back to camp. It is always better to do this immediately if at all possible. Natural predators may find and ruin your prize if you leave it, and there is also a species of human hyena which occasionally inhabits our woodlands. Such pay scant attention to deer tags.

Two of you can haul him out, if the terrain is not too rough, and you can do it by yourself if (1) he is a small deer, (2) you are in good shape, and (3) the distance is not too far. I could relate a number of tales about hauling out deer carcasses that seem pretty hilarious in retrospect even if they were perplexing enough at the time. One in particular involves a box canyon in the Kaibab, a perfectly enormous buck mule deer, and three frantic though muscular cargo handlers who very nearly didn't make it. But we did, and the venison was worth it.

If, for any of several reasons, you must leave your animal, by all means get him up off the ground and into the shade. This may not always be possible, of course, but if it isn't you are in trouble. Prop the body cavity open to speed cooling, cover him if you can and take the easiest direct route to the nearest jeep track, blazing your trail with tape which can be removed on return. Naturally go downhill—straight down the fall line—unless you can get a jeep very close to him on the uphill side. You can carry him a mile downhill easier than 200 yards uphill. If you do leave him, get back, with help and the jeep, *at once.* If it's full dark by the time you make camp, you had best wait until dawn and take your chances with the coyotes, but no later than that first streak of grey in the East. Minutes can count.

Once you have him back in camp, most of your problems are over. Not quite all, however. Hang him in the shade, skin him out, and cover him with that cheesecloth deer bag you bought where you got your license. If the weather is cold he will now be O.K. for several days, or indefinitely if it is *very* cold. When you pack up remember to protect the carcass carefully from sun, dust, gasoline, oil, paint or any other extraneous matter. If the road back is warm, drive it at night. Get your meat butchered and packed immediately on return, and freeze that which you do not plan to eat at once. Don't bother to hang it or marinate it. Prime venison taken with one clean shot doesn't need any preparation beyond that which you have already given it. Cook it as you would the best of beef (please not too long) and better eating you will not find at the fanciest restaurant in Paris.

Congratulations and *bon appétit!*

10

A
Rhineland
Roebuck

THE GERMANIC HUNTING TRADITION is very old, guided by customs that date from the Middle Ages. It is now carefully structured and, to American eyes, oddly formal. This may not be to every outdoorsman's taste, but it is necessary if hunting is to be preserved in a densely populated land. Already we see that the American system cannot survive unchanged in the age of off-road vehicles. What we do about this remains to be seen, and different conditions demand different remedies, but it is interesting to learn how the Germans have solved their problem. And they *have* solved it, for there is a great deal of game in Germany, and a great deal of hunting, despite wall-to-wall people from the Baltic to the Alps. The seasons are long, the shots are frequent, the trophies are good, the meat is on the table, and the accident rate is negligible.

The grand quarry is the *Hirsch,* a junior cousin of our wapiti. There are lots of wild boar, the chamois is coming back, and there are plenty of rabbits and birds. But the mainstay of modern German hunting is the *Reh,* or "roe deer." This is a dainty little beast running to perhaps sixty pounds dressed, smaller even than our Florida Keys deer. While the European "stag" and the American "elk" are counterparts, as are the European *"Elch"* and the American "moose," the rehbok has no new-world twin, being totally unlike our whitetails or mule deer. Though a true deer and no antelope, he is more suggestive of Africa's bushbuck than any of the deer we know.

He is all over the place now. When I sought him as a boy, back before WW II, he was somewhat scarce and one could easily be skunked on a weekend hunt. That has changed today and no tourist fails to spot scores of animals on any extended drive through the country. The danger of a crash decline is thus ever present and the game supply must be managed very carefully.

The idea that just anyone can go hunting, as long as he buys a license, is foreign to the Germans. To them a hunter is a specially qualified person, wearing certain clothes, speaking an antique jargon, observing special customs, devoted to his hobby, and carefully examined before taking the field. A man is either a *Jäger* or he is not. It is not a casual thing. To earn a hunting license *(Jagdschein)*, one must enroll in certified schools and learn all sorts of things from wildlife biology and game management to rifle marksmanship and the traditions of the chase. The curriculum is about as extensive as that of an American AA degree and normally takes a couple of years to complete, though "crash courses" are possible. The credential, once earned, is good for life. It establishes you as a qualified hunter. If you then wish to go hunting that is another matter, to be arranged between you and the custodian of a hunting concession. This man, in turn, is supervised by the game department and told how many animals of what sort must be taken from his land yearly in order to maintain a healthy balance. He owns the hunting rights, and he owns whatever meat is taken. The hunter keeps the trophy, and he may buy the meat, at current market rates, if he wishes.

This system works, and provides excellent hunting together with an abundant supply of game. It may seem rather restrictive to a wilderness hunter, but Germany is not a wilderness. It effectively eliminates the "slob hunter," enemy of us all, and it removes the need for those *iddiwa* red shirts. Wearing red, or, worse, flash orange, in the woods always makes me feel like a fool. German hunters wear green.

And so it came to pass that I was invited by my client and good friend, Fritz Gass, to come down to his concession in the Rhineland and shoot one of his rehbok. There were certain complications about my clothing and qualifications but through the courtesy of some generous officials waivers were obtained. Fritz' land lies on the left bank of the Rhine not far from Kaiserslautern, a city familiar to many American army men because of the huge base we maintain nearby. The lodge was a little doll's house in a tiny village some two hours' drive from Fritz' home. No camping, of course, was involved. This was very "civilized" hunting.

My weapon was borrowed—a Model 660 Mauser in 30-06 topped with a huge Zeiss telescope suitable for photographing the moon. Shooting a roebuck with a 30-06 is rather like shooting a man with a 20 mm. It will certainly suffice, but seems a bit much. (I zeroed 2-inches high at 100 yards with 150-grain, flat-base, spitzer soft-points.)

Shooting is mainly from stands in this region, and one can see the *Hochsitze* scattered throughout the countryside, generally at the edge of the forest overlooking a glade. A hochsitz is a two-passenger platform, with sides and roof, perched twelve to twenty feet in the air on log stilts. It is usually made of raw pine and weathered to a dull grey. Inside it, one sits on a plank and rests his rifle on the rail. The shooting sling is of little value here and is not seen on European sporting rifles.

Deer are crepuscular creatures everywhere, and since we had driven down and moved in after lunch we had the evening twilight for our first sortie. We set forth at about five-thirty, installed in a forest-green Mercedes 450 sedan—roughing it all the way. This was hobbit country—rolling green hills in which stands of forest alternated with meadows. Small crofts set in neatly tilled fields dotted the range, joined by smooth, unpaved roads. Wild shooting poses no hazard to the farmers because there is no wild shooting. The man in green with the Tyroler hat and the scoped rifle can be depended upon to use his weapon with care.

Hawks of various kinds were common, and great placid hares hopped about with curious deliberation.

We glide to a stop within a pine copse on a hillside above a particularly picturesque dale.

"Wir mussen nun sehr still bleiben!" whispers Fritz. *"Schhhh!"*

O.K. Very quiet. I carefully do not slam the door as I dismount.

My unseemly khaki work clothes are concealed beneath a borrowed green loden cloak, and my dark brown felt hat, though not regulation, is still not conspicuous. We move down toward the hochsitz in Indian fashion—not to snap a twig! The rifle feels pleasantly purposeful in my hands. Holding a rifle, to a hunter, is something like holding a baby is to a mother.

Now up in the box, we wait. What a lovely wait! We are far from the Vienna Woods, but I am minded of Strauss' opening bars.

The light dims. Presently a doe and three fawns appear through the wheat over the rise to our left. They move out into the mown hay, delicate and charming. After a bit Fritz barks like a fox and they scurry off. We don't want them to complicate the situation.

It is now seven o'clock. We have perhaps 15 minutes of light left. Nothing today?

Then there is a faint flash of tan high up on the cut pine slope across the brook. I put the glass on it as Fritz uses his binoculars. It's a buck, but very far—some 400 meters. He's coming down to drink. The range closes.

At 250 I whisper, *"Gut genug?"* Will he do? Fritz grins and nods. Now he will show me something.

As the buck reaches the stream Fritz calls him. The cry doesn't sound like anything I can identify, but it works—like a charm. Without hesitation the beast raises his head and trots toward the sound. He stops. Fritz calls again, and on he comes.

"Jetzt?" Now? Fritz says nothing. I can shoot anytime now but Fritz wants to show me just how close he can call a deer.

I cannot judge the range. The animal is of an odd size, the light is dim, and the big glass, set on 6X, is mounted so far aft that I cannot see around it. But he is close. Too close. This is too much like assassination!

Then he scents us. Alarm, head up, and away!

Now the musical accompaniment, which has been Beethoven's Pastoral Symphony, shifts to the Gipsy Baron as the buck bounds through the woods like the flicker of a moonbeam on a windy night. Across the meadow, through that little stand of pines, one arching leap over the brook and up the bank beyond. The reticle tracks him but I reject any thought of a snap shot. I am the guest for whom this whole production has been staged. As a professional shottist I must not boggle the scene with a sloppy shot! I will pass up the opportunity rather than miss, or, much worse, wound. Now the whole thing is up to him. If he keeps going he's safe.

The curse of Lot's wife dooms the deer. On the far ridge, four times as far from us as he was a moment before, he stops and looks back. The Mauser has a sweet trigger—three pounds, crisp and motionless. I allow one second for a compressed surprise break. I honestly don't believe the buck heard the shot.

Bolt open. Unload. Lens caps on.

Fritz extends his hand.

"Waidmanns Heil!" The German word for "hunter" is *Jäger*, but to a German hunter a brother hunter is a *Waidmann*.

We clasp hands.

"*Waidmanns Dank!*" I answer, in accordance with the old formula. We formally tip our hats, to each other, and then to the deer.

It is almost full dark now, but we wait to hear the waldhorns sounding from the distance, questing and responding. A buck has fallen, and all who know the calls can tell. It is all very solemn, formal, and correct.

The head was very nice, fully developed and prime with three points on each side. The animal was a four-year-old, and the records begin at five, but considering that this was the first buck we saw we were well satisfied. It was, of course, much too dark for natural-light photos.

We performed the prescribed rituals—the last bite, the hat sprig, the blood mark—and took the carcass to a spot where the viscera could be left for fox bait before we dressed it. Foxes are something of a nuisance to the farmers and varminting is appreciated. Naturally I recovered the liver, kidneys, and the undamaged heart. (I have long since abandoned the heart shot as it does not anchor well, and have coincidentally saved much good meat.) Since the venison belonged to Fritz anyway I generously let him keep it (big of me, hey?), but we all dined luxuriously later that night on this-day-fresh venison liver, one of the world's chief delicacies.

On our way in we met various farmers out on the road in the headlights, cheerily offering us their *Waidmanns Heils,* but the stylistic touch was reserved for Hans, who was the other gun in our party and had been stationed a mile or so distant in another hochsitz.

"I did not wait for the horn, but lifted my hat when I heard the shot," he said. "I knew the Herr Oberst would kill clean."

Nicely put, but I wish my confidence in my marksmanship were as great as his.

The antlers now hang on my wall beneath another pair I collected in 1937 near Zell-am-See in Austria. Forty-one years between roebucks! It's not the size of the trophy that matters, it is the consciousness it recalls of an event worth remembering. In Ortega's excellent words, "*No se caza para matar, sino, al revés, se mata para haber cazado.*"* This German hunt was orchestrated like a minuet, with everything in order and cleanly executed. As the Japanese say of such a happening, "*That* was a poem."

---

*"*One does not hunt in order to kill. One kills in order to have hunted.*"*

11

The Fall
of the Wild

THE MODERN GLOBE TROTTER is generally a sheltered type. This superficial paradox may be due to the fact that in our present culture only sheltered types seem to make enough money to go travelling. Or again, it may be that the market for travel tales is made up of tube-watchers who presumably demand a lot of ooh-ing and ah-ing, phony or not, in order to keep up their increasingly sluggish circulation. In either case there is a tendency to point out the marvelous skills of, shall we say, "underdeveloped" citizens—skills which must awe and bewilder the more civilized observer.

In this matter I am alternately amused and perplexed by travelers' accounts of the wit, skill, prowess, courage and woodcraft of various exotic local boys. In my own wanderings I seem to have met all the wrong people. Admitting that the Eskimo hunts whales in a kayak, and that the Nandi kill lions with spears, and that Abebe Bikela seems to have been the world's greatest distance runner, the assumption that any native sportsman you run across in the backwoods of the world is necessarily a combination of Daniel Boone and Jed Smith is apt to lead to some ludicrous situations.

I'm thinking of an occurrence not long ago on the Rio Ixcán, in the wilderness of northern Guatemala. Our party was composed of three "culturally advanced" Anglo-Saxon types and four local residents, the latter of Maya and Lacandón stock. As I sat in the shade of a palm-branch lean-to, checking my equipment after our customary dawn prowl, I became conscious of the distant barking of a dog. It came from the general direction of some small rancherías we had noted earlier, so it did not seem consequential to me. But it had a curious effect on Luís, one of our Mayas. It lighted some obscure fires in his dim personality. He trotted up to me manifesting a sort of lethargic enthusiasm, or excited apathy. This is tough to manifest, but it is an attribute of the modern Maya. It may be the principal attribute of the modern Maya.

"*¡Tepiscuintle!*" he said. "*¡Tepiscuintle!*" Exclamations are more exclamatory when you precede them with an inverted exclamation point. Latin Americans do it all the time.

"*¿Estás seguro?*" I asked. "Are you sure?"

"*¡Sí, tepiscuintle. Muy buena para comer!*"

Now tepiscuintle is the Maya name for a capybara (does that help?) and this was a beastie I especially wanted to meet. It is something like a mixture of giant guinea pig and giant muskrat. It is partially aquatic and is supposed to inhabit holes along the banks of rivers. Its meat is said to be one of the great delicacies of the world. One friend of mine who knows Central America well told me that one can even make a delicious sandwich out of the skin. *¡Muy buena para comer!*

I had no notion of how Luís could tell that this particular dog had actually run a tepiscuintle to earth, but it was his country, in which I was a stranger, and I had to assume that he knew more about such things than I.

"*Bueno. Vámonos. Pronto.*" As the others were occupied and there seemed no need to make a production out of harvesting an oversized rodent, no matter how toothsome, I told Luís to lead on and the two of us immediately moved out, homing on the still barking dog. I took nothing but my pistol, which is perfectly adequate for anything and any range likely in those parts, while Luís had his machete. Our direction was approximately northwest.

The river at that point is bordered by a dense growth of wild cane, which is not easy to penetrate. Almost at once we had to resort to hands and knees, Luís leading and cutting with no special dexterity at the tangle. He had a knack for cutting the wrong branch, so that the stroke opened a bit of scenery ahead without making passage any easier, and then crawling under the actual obstruction.

I am not usually nervous about snakes, but this groveling around in a canebrake, too close to the ground and still without being able to see it, was just a touch spooky. Also it was hot and sweaty. I've enjoyed some other hunts more.

It might be well to mention at this point that we met no snakes, then or ever. Though I have spent much time in regions supposedly "infested" with poisonous snakes— the *barba amarilla*, or fer-de-lance, is reputedly very fond of canebrakes, for instance— I just don't have any luck in actually finding them. In nearly a dozen different ventures into the wilds of tropical America, the only venomous snake I ever saw was a small, dead corali, stomped into the trail by a mule.

After about three hundred yards we were through the cane and into a form of scrub jungle, somewhat more open, but harder to cut through. This increased Luís' problems, which were already almost too much for him. The dog continued to bark, closer now, and we continued on course 315°.

About a quarter mile from camp we came upon the dog, a small, black, undernourished specimen bouncing in circles among the trees and yelping excitedly. Luís, with visions of tepiscuintle evidently dancing in his head, at once began rummaging around looking for the hole. It didn't get through to him that the dog was looking up, not down. We were also quite a long way from any river bank. But Luís persisted. Gotta be a hole around here somewhere!

Though perfectly willing to grant superior knowledge of local conditions to the natives, I at length felt called upon to point out that what the dog had bayed was a small and exasperated brown squirrel, which for some reason seemed to want to stay in his chosen tree rather than simply to flit off through the canopy.

"*Es una ardilla, no mas. No mas grande que un ratón,*" I said. A squirrel, no bigger than a mouse.

"*Ah,*" said Luís. "*Verdad.*" A long silence. Then in a tone of dubious optimism, "*Muy buena para comer.*"

Feeling more than slightly irritated at this demonstration of the lore of the jungle, I lapsed into English.

"No doubt, Tarzan. But, assuming I could hit that jittery chipmunk up there in the treetops, and assuming that a 45 caliber wadcutter would leave enough of him to make the pan smell, I somehow can't see myself returning to camp in triumph with a squirrel—and that about one-third the size of the squirrels that live in my own backyard at home. No, thanks."

"*¿Señor?*" Questions also gain a little something in the Spanish mode.

"*No necesitamos ardillas. Vamos al encampamento.*"

"*Muy bien, pues . . .*" And then, under his breath, "*Muy buena para comer.*"

He knew I was crazy, of course. Anyone who would hike three days into a howling wilderness, to sleep on the ground and soak alternately in sweat and rain, to be bitten by bugs and live on a diet of black beans and instant coffee, is obviously out of his head. But, for my part, I was beginning to wonder a bit about *him.* My wonder quickly gave way to certainty. This lad was not about to replace Hiawatha.

The proof was beautiful in its simplicity. Luís shrugged, looked around vaguely, and pointed with his machete to the northwest, cutting his hand on a thorn in the process.

I thought he had sighted game. It didn't occur to me that he meant that we should proceed back to camp by continuing in the direction we had come. We could, come to think of it, have done it that way—in about ten years—but it hardly seemed the best method under the circumstances.

"*¿Venado?*" You see a deer?

"*Venado no hay. Encampamento.*"

It was clear that he had got himself disoriented while looking for the tepiscuintle hole. I made a dispirited attempt to be tactful. Calling him a blithering idiot to his face would not accomplish anything, and besides I don't know how to say "blithering" in Spanish. To the southwest, about 90° from our line of travel and some fifty yards off, I could see sky through the edge of the canopy. There were cornfields around—

the dog had come from such a place—and it was at least likely that this was one. Having no taste for retracing our squirm through the canebrake, I pointed toward the clearing.

"*Hay una milpa allá.*" The local term for a cornfield is "*milpa.*" "*Vamos por acá.*"

Luís looked even more depressed than usual. He clearly did not relish being lost in the forest with a crazy gringo who wouldn't even shoot a meal when it was right in front of him. He did, however, make a kind of attempt. Alvarado had come through this country some 400 years ago, establishing a deep-rooted tradition of compliance with foreigners. Luís got untangled, pointed himself in the direction I indicated, and took half-a-dozen listless swings at the brush with his machete. He then looked dolefully at me and pronounced, like the Grand Inquisitor abandoning a heretic to the secular arm: "*No hay milpa.*"

I was beginning to see what had become of the ancient Maya. Nothing. But I did want to get back to camp. It was now midday and the idea of a swim in the cool, green river was most attractive. As Luís was absolutely no help, it was clear that I'd better make it on my own. With no machete, this was not simple. (I'd no more ask an Indian for his machete than he would ask me for my pistol. Some things are not done.) However, jungle is rarely "impenetrable" except just at its edges and such was the case here. I could walk erect, though with some difficulty, to within about fifteen yards of the edge of the milpa. At that point I resorted to the rhinoceros system. You take off your sombrero, lower your head, lead with one shoulder, and charge. On perhaps the tenth charge I burst out into the open and fell flat on my back, feeling ragged, filthy, and out of sorts. But it really was a cornfield, and under the open sky the terrain pattern was obvious. The cultivated land was bordered to my left by a line of tall trees marking a tributary watercourse, dry at this season, which led almost directly to our camp on the main stream.

Well, anyway, it was obvious to me. It wasn't to Luís. After I had declined to follow his directions I thought that he would possibly try them himself, but either out of loneliness or some rudimentary and misguided sense of responsibility, he opted to follow me. When I crashed out into the milpa, I looked back to see him standing in the tunnel I had just created, dangling his machete.

"If you say, '*Muy buena para comer,*' amigo, I may just feed you to the piranhas," I muttered to myself. "You and they have the same tastes."

Luís felt the need to reestablish his woodcraft. He nodded in friendly fashion to suggest that here indeed was a cornfield. It was the sort of thing that we could agree on.

"*Aqui hay milpa. Allá el encampamento,*" and he pointed directly away from camp.

It was really pretty fascinating. I imagine that even a total stranger to New York City, granted a clear day, would not try to reach the Empire State Building by going north from Central Park. And yet here was this backwoods Indian proposing a course just about as sensible. Rather than philosophize, however, I just brushed myself off and said, "*Vamos, pues.*" "Pues" is a word used in Central America as a sort of spacer. It may be equivalent to "well" or "then," but again it may not. To one at loss for words, as I was, it is a godsend.

There was not much more to the episode. I plodded back to camp with Luís dogging my heels. On two further occasions he pointed the way. Instead of being 180° out, however, he was closer to 90°. This could be considered an improvement, by a sociologist.

The question arises as to how this lad could survive by himself in the bush. Since he had no motive for being deliberately wrong, I must assume that he had no more sense of direction than a toy balloon, and yet he had grown up in this wilderness, to which I was a stranger. My only conclusion is that the wild forests of Central America constitute a friendly environment, in which getting lost is not a matter of great consequence, at least if you are an Indian with nothing much else to do. There is quite a lot to eat, water is no problem, the climate is mild, and there are enough little farm plots scattered throughout to insure that you are seldom more than a couple of hours' walk from somebody.

It is certainly possible that this particular experience was an exception, but if so I must just naturally attract the exceptions. I have had quite a number of similar adventures, and for me the competent local has been the exception. It would be foolish to assume from this that there are no good woodsmen in the backlands, for there must be. The error is in generalization. Excellence is always exceptional. Everybody you know drives a car; how many drive one really well? Thus it must be with native woodcraft: Be glad if it's there but don't be surprised if it's not.

12

AGUARDIENTES DE AGAVE

As A LEGACY FROM MY FATHER, who was a gourmet of parts, I prize a firm belief in the Principle of Adaptation, most particularly in matters of gastronomy. He taught that one eats lobster in Maine and abalone in California, not vice-versa. He urged that one drink stout in Ireland and lager in Bavaria; burgundy in France and sherry in Spain.

Extending this policy to continents, it has always struck me as peculiar that, in the matter of beverages, we Yankees have been rather unimaginative. We have brought our drinks with us from the Old World and sought to transplant them—which is worthy enough—but in doing so we have traditionally scorned the liquid contributions of our predecessors, the American Indians. And these deserve better of us.

This is not to suggest that all aspects of neolithic American culture are universally adaptable to our present way of life—dog, boiled whole without salt, does not appeal— but the people who gave us potatoes, tomatoes, maize, beans, avocados, and chilies for our table clearly made possible the cuisine now used by the entire world. And in their *aguardientes de agave*—the spirits of the maguey—they have also given us a native beverage which, while traditionally enjoyed in Mexico, has only recently begun to be appreciated by us Norteños.

"Agave americana" is called the American aloe, the century plant, the maguey, or simply the agave. (I see by the dictionary that it is permissible to pronounce this uh-GAY-vee, but I prefer the more melodic Spanish ah-gah-VAY.) It is native of Mexico and the Southwestern U.S. but it has been introduced into the Mediterranean world for both ornamental and hedging purposes. Its fierce gray spines make a formidable fence, and its fibers make excellent cordage, but in this discussion we are more interested in its juice.

The milky white sap, drawn directly from the living heart, has a pleasant tart-sweet flavor. Curiously, it lathers and is sometimes used as a detergent. When fermented it is called *pulque,* or specifically *pulque de maguey,* since there are other pulques made from various fruits, particularly the melons. Pulque de maguey is a mild, sparkling drink, vaguely reminiscent of hard cider. Its alcoholic content is about that of light beer—say, 6%. Like cider, its quality depends entirely on the care used by the producer, and the drink has much in common with the little girl with the little curl in the middle of her forehead.

It is possible to produce a spirit by distilling pulque, just as a sort of whiskey may be made by distilling beer, but contrary to general belief this is not how tequila is achieved. Tequila (note the single "l"—no "y" sound involved) and mezcal are the spirits of the agave, and they are made by distilling a mash made from the cooked hearts of young plants, not a fermented juice.

The terminology used by the Mexicans in these matters is no less confusing to the layman than that of whiskey distillers. *Aguardiente,* or "ardent water," is the general term for distilled spirits—as *Schnapps* is in German—and both tequila and mezcal fall into this classification. However, tequila is made in the town of Tequila, Jalisco, while mezcal is made in the South, with principal distilleries in the state of Oaxaca and headquartered at Mitla, a village otherwise known for its impressive Zapotec antiquities. In the South the drink itself is called mezcal, while in Jalisco mezcal is the term for the cooked heart of the plant, which is eaten as a confection if any can be pilfered on its way to the crushing mill. The two distillates are quite similar, the slight difference in flavor being due to climate and soil factors rather than to essential variation in production methods. Thus the bottled end-products differ as Scotch whiskey does from Irish, not as whiskey does from brandy.

The manufacture of tequila commences with the somewhat barbarous process of ripping the whole six-year-old plant out of the ground. This seems extravagant at first thought, but it is really more in harmony with the economy of Mexico than otherwise, for in Jalisco there is practically no limit on space or labor supply, and the unending fields of maguey are never diminished enough to notice.

The uprooted plant is then trimmed down to its heart, the sword-like leaves going to the fiber plant and any suckers being saved for replanting. The hearts, three to four feet long and some twenty inches thick, are split once, lengthwise, packed into brick ovens, and blasted with live steam until the ivory-white pulp is the color of cream sherry.

The cooking softens the tough heart fibers, and when an oven is opened any lurking urchins are quick to risk scorched fingers for a taste of the rich, brown contents. To a northern palate the result tastes something like a ripe quince.

The cooked pulp is transferred to a macerating machine, sometimes a modern grinding mill and sometimes a mule-powered stone wheel. There are fifteen distilleries in Tequila and methods vary. At the San Matthias plant a team of mules circles a central pivot, trundling a six-foot stone rolling on a radius beam, while an attendant shovels the resulting mash from the edges of the pit back to its center.

Fibers are mostly screened out at the mill and the thick, liquid residue is piped to vats where it ferments. When sugar content is reduced and specific gravity indicates sufficient natural alcohol, the mash is double-distilled, cut to market proof (about 90) and flows forth, gin-clear, as *tequila nacida.*

At the distilleries, a visitor is sometimes invited to try a horn of uncut tequila, smoking hot from the still. This is supposed to produce a violent reaction something like biting into a fresh Jalapeño chile, but if the sampler turns never a hair he is regarded as a man of valor.

Like any other new spirit, raw tequila is harsh, but aging and grading can produce a beverage of any desired quality. As the aging takes place in wood casks, the tequila *añejo* (from the Spanish año, meaning year) takes on a pale amber color, varying according to the type of each maker's casks. Certain producers introduce a maguey worm—an Aztec delicacy—into a bottle of aged tequila. It's possible that my palate is insufficiently sensitive, but I can detect no effect on flavor attributable to this entomological condiment, and thus lay the whole thing to an attempt to startle *turistas.*

As a means of getting drunk, tequila has no rival, simply because of its price. A liter of the new runs seven pesos at the distillery, while excellent aged spirits cost nine pesos. Choice reserves, for special bottling, are somewhat higher, but never comparable to whiskey, brandy or gin. Even in competition with local rum, tequila enjoys a 50 to 100% cost edge.

As a beverage, tequila (and at the risk of offending some Tapatío friends, you may read "mezcal" for "tequila" if you wish) has the simultaneous advantage and disadvantage of a strong, distinctive flavor. It is not for the vodka drinkers who want effect without taste, and I suspect it is not for those who fancy the lightest possible Scotch or the thinner bourbons. Tequila "comes through" like a good Irish whiskey, and if you want to disguise your potations you probably won't like it.

On the other hand, those who prefer dark beer to light, who like a fish that tastes of the sea and not the poultry loft, and who relish the muscular savor of venison and wild duck—such people will regard tequila as a splendid and neighborly liquor, appropriate for all purposes to which spirits may properly be put.

Because of its odd and penetrating flavor tequila does not usually mix well, any more than Scotch does. The customary condiments, used with customary alcohols, such as fruit juices, patent soft drinks, and spiced wines, are often defeated and confounded by the vigor of the maguey. Consequently, tequila is most often and most properly drunk straight. Traditionally lime juice is taken as an enhancer—and salt seems more appropriate than sugar.

However, various experiments along the daiquiri line have been tried, and any formula you fancy using tequila or mezcal as the spirit, lime juice as the acid, and bar syrup, grenadine, honey or your favorite cordial as the sweet may work out to your taste. A good starting formula on which to base your lab work is 3-2-1, implying three parts spirit, two parts sour, one part sweet. Always add a dash of salt to the result.

Tequila makes an admirable boilermaker, particularly if a good *dark* beer is used, such as the excellent and popular Dos Equis of Mexico. Tequila and Dos Equis should properly be called the Mexican boilermaker.

The juice of the pomegranate is favored in Jalisco, if tequila must be mixed. Ponche de Granada is a holiday favorite in Guadalajara.

In the Sierra de Juárez, in Lower California, I was introduced to another odd mixture—this time equal parts of strong black coffee and tequila. The two powerful flavors blend curiously well, and the mixture may be termed Café Juárez, in honor of the range, not the great man, who was rather abstemious in such matters.

It is also possible to make a martini with tequila, though it's hard to approve of this custom of using the name of one drink to designate another which is totally different, by merely prefixing its title with the name of another base. (A "vodka-martini," for example, may be a good drink but it is *not* a martini and should not be so called.) If a cold tequila-plus-dash-of-vermouth drink is attempted, an eighth-lime wedge should be used in place of olive or onion, and the glass rimmed with salt.

But my favorite tequila concoction does not even contain tequila—it is drunk separately, in alternate sips. It is a very Aztec-type affair, and if its ingredients astonish you all I can say is, "Try it—it's good!" It is called "sangrita" and it's made of orange juice, tomato juice, sugar, salt and chile! Outstanding!

RECIPES

MARGARITA
>2 parts tequila or mezcal
>1 part lime juice
>1 part triple-sec or curaçao
>Blend with ice and serve in salt-rimmed glass

BERTA
>2 ounces tequila
>1 ounce lime juice
>1 teaspoon sugar
>Dash with orange bitters, pour over cracked ice in a long glass and fill with soda

JARABE *(Tequila-Martini)*
>5 parts tequila
>1 part dry Vermouth or domestic equivalent
>Dash with orange bitters, mix with ice cubes, and pour off into chilled glass
>>containing lime wedge and rimmed with salt

CAFÉ JUÁREZ
>Equal parts of tequila and strong black coffee, served very hot

MEXICAN BOILERMAKER
>1 bottle dark Mexican beer, very cold
>2 ounces tequila
>Drink alternately

SANGRITA *(non-alcoholic tequila chaser)*
>1 quart orange juice
>½ quart tomato juice
>2 tablespoons sugar
>1½ teaspoons salt
>¼ teaspoon Tabasco sauce (or to taste)
>>(This could replace alcohol!)

13

The
First
Race

T HE RAIN WAS HOLDING OFF and by 9 A.M. a few patches of blue were showing toward the west. The course would be dry and there would be no glare unless the overcast thinned too much. He felt excited and afraid and proud. After watching and talking and trying to learn what no teachers can impart, he was at last a competitor, a pilot. His license said so, his name was on the program, his car had been passed by the technical inspectors and carried a large red number "40" on its white skin.

He stood in the door of the hangar where the small cars were garaged. A smell of petroleum and a clamor of tuning engines carried past him out to where the bleachers were beginning to show a few customers.

The airport wore a festive air. Parking was becoming a problem and vendors of soft drinks and other oddments were in evidence. Every other person seemed to wear some sort of official badge. Car crews and drivers milled around, tinkering with the cars and chattering continuously in an arcane jargon.

Various expensive looking women, apparently worried about what they should have worn instead of what they were wearing, appeared to be attached to the crews of the more impressive cars.

Amateur officials strove earnestly to bring organization to a host of unorganized, individualistic, amateur contestants, and to a much larger mob of curious and equally unorganized spectators, including a startling number of raucous small boys.

Periodically, a beautiful, shining dream of an automobile would shoulder its way to or from the service area, with much revving of its engine to avoid the indignities of plug fouling due to low engine speed. A horn was not necessary since the open exhausts announced themselves without reticence to anyone in the way.

"This is really a damfool trick," he thought. "I can't afford it. I can't drive against these rich boys with their Italian machinery and their imported mechanics and their trailers. If I burn anything out on the little bus God knows how I'll pay for it. Besides, I'm scaring Laurie to death and right now I don't feel so good myself."

He went back into the hangar. His wife and the two friends who made up his crew were primping the little car with anxious affection. In practice it had seemed perfect except for a faint uneasiness in the clutch, but everyone was trying to remember some forgotten precaution which might be decisive.

"Anything more?"

"I don't know what it would be. We've set up the clutch and brake pedals. We've set the valves and gapped the plugs. We've checked all belts and nuts. And I've just finished wiring down everything that can work loose. I think I've got it built."

"That's wonderful. I don't know why you guys go to all this trouble, but I guess you know how much I appreciate it."

"Forget it. It's all on account of your beautiful wife. You know what the Doctor says about friends of the family."

He grinned and went around where Laurie was wiping the last bit of polish off the sleek, white hood. She was wearing blue denim yachting clothes and had a large smudge of grease on her forehead.

"About time to roll it out, Sugar. Think it will bear the family colors with honor?"

"It better! After all this trouble. If it lets you down now I'll kick it right in the differential!"

He whispered. "How do you feel?"

"I'm O.K. How do *you* feel?"

"Butterflies. But they'll go away. It says here."

"Don't worry about anything, Darling. About me or anything. I'm having a marvelous time." But she wasn't.

"Sure," he said.

The first race, *his* race, was set for 10:30. Seventy-six miles, 20 times around the 3.8 mile circuit. It was about half on the runways of the airport and half on the approach roads in the now unused barracks area. It had one long fast straight, two fast bends, and the usual array of right angles and hairpins. A good course, varied, fun to drive and reasonably visible to the "paying guests." The Ferrari of the aristocracy lapped it in somewhat less than three minutes. The best he had done in practice was 3 minutes 29 seconds. But he wasn't racing against them, and besides he had never really pushed it in practice.

By 10 o'clock the pit crews were on station, the public address system was playing a scratchy march tune, and most of the cars seemed ready. It looked as if the race might actually start on time. He had warmed the car carefully and it had felt wonderful. Its clean, sharp, four-cylinder crackle sang with vitality and the promise of power. As he had rolled it gently out of the hangar and across to the starting position, he could feel its quick, hard liveliness even at a crawl. Confidence flowed into him from its wheel, its pedals, its bucket seat.

At the pit area he pulled on the gloves and the hard, white helmet. Then he quickly slipped the helmet off again, feeling foolish. More than ten minutes to go.

"You're not supposed to be able to spit," he thought.

He went some yards into the infield grass and, after some difficulty, spat lustily. He felt quite pleased with himself until he saw that Laurie had been watching him. He walked back to her.

"*Are* you all right?" she asked quietly.

"Sure, sure, sure. After all, this is the first time. A man's apt to be a little edgy. Honest, I feel fine—considering everything."

The fear was not exactly logical. Statistically he was safer than on a turnpike. Bent metal was not uncommon, but death or serious injury was.

No, it was more like the feeling on a roller coaster—the ecstatic, terrifying thrill of violent motion. But here it was magnified by the insistent stimulation of the roaring engine and the sense of mastery over unimaginable force—force which submitted sweetly to skill but could turn savagely against an incompetent master.

"You take it easy, Hero. You don't have to win anything. Remember, this is for fun."

"Well, yes. But it wouldn't be fun if I didn't try. But don't fret, Sugar. I don't want to bend anything trying, least of all the breadwinner."

The others joined them.

"Don't worry about the OSCAs. You can't touch them and maybe they'll blow up if they race each other enough. You try to stay ahead of that 36 till the turn. I don't think he can pass you, but then you probably can't pass him either once the parade lines up."

"Where does he start?"

"He's one row behind you but they're staggered so he can jump you if you let him."

"Right. Where is that 27? He looked pretty ardent in practice."

"Four rows back. I don't think he can touch you unless you get excited and goof it somewhere. He just hasn't the torque. He gets those lap times by cowboying through the corners."

"I doubt if he's going to slide by me in a turn. I seem to be using all of the available road."

"Well he won't if you stay *on* the road. Just don't take them any faster than possible—what could be simpler?"

"O.K. And to hell with this strategy business. I'm going to get up as far in the pack as I can and stay there. First lap. So don't bother to signal unless something is wrong or all the competition drops out."

"O.K., Nuvolari. Enjoy yourself."

"Good luck, Maestro. Don't terrorize the peasantry."

He kissed Laurie briefly. She looked trim and lovely in spite of the grease and the worry.

"Good luck, Darling. Don't get mad."

"You're my luck, Angel. Don't forget to wave."

He kissed her again, harder, then walked quickly over to the car, put on his helmet, and got in. He locked the quick-release belt across his lap. He switched on the ignition, checked his instruments, and turned it off. He sat and waited. He began to talk himself cool, as he had done years before on his first hunting trips. "Take it easy, Sport. Nothing hinges on this. You're out here for fun. Relax and enjoy it. The car is good but don't overdo it. Keep that tach needle where it belongs, use your brakes where it counts, keep that power on in the drifts, and don't try anything exotic. Easy does it. No sweat. Relax--------"

His concentration was splintered by the voice from the speaker.

"Start your engines!"

He switched the key and touched the starter. The wonderful sound, joyful as a trumpet call, washed away his nervousness with a flood of eager excitement. He cracked the engine hard, twice, checked his oil pressure, then glanced up toward the starter on his perch. The starter was holding up his hand, waiting for each driver to return the signal which means "Engine running—ready!" He raised his left arm, suddenly dropped it to set his goggles in place, then raised it again.

There was a black car on his right, blue on his left. To his right front another blue, to his left front, a flame red. There was space for him to pass between, if he could.

The green flag was up. He turned the engine up to 4,000. One—two—three—SOCK IT!

The air exploded with a fantastic clamor of howling engines and squealing rubber. He was pressed back against the seat as the whole pack rocketed forward together. In first gear, to 4,500—in second, to 5,000. He was moving up between the blue and the red. In third to 5,000. He was between them. Ahead, two sleek coupes, one green, one maroon—and ahead of them, the two flying OSCAs, already in the fast left bend.

Now in fourth gear, flat out, he did not close on the coupes, and behind he caught the flash of a blue and white car—number 36—his competition.

Into the bend, his throttle on the floorboards, he hoped the red car to his left was clear, and then almost before he could wonder he was into the first corner, 90° to the right.

Damn! Out of position. Keep the head busy. You know, like old T.J. Think! Well, drag it through, don't sit and gripe!

The error threw him slightly too wide, not out of control but fighting for it, and 36 smoothly pulled up on his right.

He was in charge again and let the engine wind higher than safe in third in order

to pull ahead of the blue and white. There was no time for fourth as he set himself for the next corner. This time he was right, with three-fourths of a length and the better angle on 36. Hard on the brake—don't lock the wheels, just—keep that tach needle up—down into second—now, blast it through! Woops, 6,000 in second! Easy, you've got him now. Don't burn anything out with a stupid mistake.

Out of third at 5,000. Get over to the right, there's nobody alongside. Now, two 45° lefts. Watch it, you green coupe! You've got to do better than that or get out of my way. Down to third and link the two 45's in one long, smooth drift. That's got it— and the green car, too! Now he's between me and old 36. Just the maroon car ahead and the two OSCAs somewhere off in front.

He held position well through a quarter circle to the right and another 90° right and was on the back straight. Long—smooth—straight. The engine's clear resonant baritone rose slowly to tenor. The tach needle slanted toward the end of the dial. Maroon in front, white and green in the middle, blue and white behind—100, 110, 115, 118 miles per hour. No change in position. Long—smooth—straight.

And here is the end of it! Don't worry about these other guys, remember your brake point. Not yet—not yet. My God, look at it come! And—now! Stand on it, boy! Throw it right into second, around the hairpin in a wild slide at 4,000 RPM, then up the short straight toward the pit curve.

He had gained a little on the maroon coupe, and as they drifted out of the bend he was less than a length behind at the pits. He remembered to signal "O.K." with his hand like a Ballantine's ad as he flashed past the pit with the big black "40" numerals on it.

For three laps these positions held, and already the OSCAs, thirty yards apart, were commencing to lap the rear of the field.

Then something parted in the maroon car and it fell rapidly back through the pack, dismally blowing smoke from its twin exhausts.

"Well, I'll be damned!" he thought. "I'm in front! Except, of course, for the Maserati brothers."

"But I can't do anything wrong, or ease off. Those two sports are too close."

Number 36 and the green coupe were having a fierce race about 50 yards behind him, and alternated leading past the pits for five more laps.

Then, on the back straight, the OSCAs cruised by with some 20 miles per hour to spare. The pilot of the second one waved to him as he went by.

"O.K., friend, enjoy yourself. Us common people have fun, too." He waved back.

On the twelfth lap the clutch, which had been gently suggesting a more sedate pace for some time, began to show distinct signs of distress. It no longer took hold with that solid, comforting shock, and his pit signals told him that he was taking one second longer each time around.

On the fifteenth lap the green coupe pulled firmly past him coming out of the hairpin, and 36 was nearly abreast as they passed the pits.

He tried to remember his own counsel. "Easy does it. It's just for fun. Nobody *has* to win." But when 36, having dropped back on two 90°corners, easily accelerated past him coming out of the second, he began to feel his disappointment and exasperation pouring through the widening chinks in his self-control.

"It's got to be the corners! Farther into them and don't drop those revs. Watch it, 36! You can't shut off that far out and stay ahead! Next time and I'll take you—and this is the time! That's right, 36, hit the old brakes right there! Now—watch how it's done. Right by here, and across, now brake, now shift—and—there!"

He was so exhilarated by this exploit that he lost both his pain at the slipping clutch *and* his caution. On the one-lap-to-go signal, hoping to hold for the finish and hard pressed by 36, he hit the linked 45's with about 3 miles per hour too many.

As the rear wheels began to ooze out of line to the right, and he gently brought the wheel in his hands to dead center, centrifugal force suddenly took over and he was gone. He snapped the wheel hard to the right but he might have been sliding on glare ice for all the effect it had. His mind seemed very clear. He noted, as the car turned crosswise to the track, that 36 was far enough back to miss him. He saw 27, the other pre-race problem, just a little farther back. To his right he saw the green coupe fish-tailing wildly and took some satisfaction in realizing that it too had taken the turn too fast, due to his pressure. But the green car was going to make it. He was not.

As the spin continued he was for an instant pointing directly at 36, sliding under brakes to avoid him, then, both clutch and brake pedals hard down, he broadsided neatly between two of the course-marking barrels into the infield, coming to rest, engine still running, in a cloud of rubber smoke.

Numbers 36 and 27 were gone in an instant. Without thought he shifted quickly to low and flung the little car around to the left to return by the same gap through which he had spun. He had no conscious feeling of fear, dismay, or anger, but his hands were shaking violently.

A black car appeared to his left, but there was time. He saw the flagman wave him in and lunged back on the course, accelerating as rapidly as his sick clutch would permit.

"Well, that does it. Where am I now? Sixth or maybe seventh if you count the OSCAs—no better than fourth even if you don't. Hell, whoever said you could drive? All right, shut up! You're not hurt—you didn't even clobber a barrel—and if you don't quit you can catch that 27 on the straight. Get on it, boy! Take this one easy and then pour it on down the runway.

"And there he is. Little red 27—maybe 50 yards ahead. At least the clutch holds in fourth. Closing—closing. Two lengths—one. There—I can see his instruments. Come on, Baby, we're running out of road! 5,500, 5,600, 5,700 on the tach. Abreast, now—and there comes the shut-off point. We've—just—about—got it. Got it! GOT IT! Now through the hairpin, with much tire noise from 27 trying furiously to make it up in this, the last tight corner. He's close—less than a length—but he won't make it now, even with this damned clutch."

And then, in a mental double take, he realized what he had seen on that hairpin turn and had been too busy to understand. The two OSCAs, one red, one black, parked off in the grass, with an ugly looking rent along one gleaming, crimson flank.

How long had they been there! He seemed to remember more than one lap. Hey, where are we now!

He took the last bend into the finish with his foot hard down, raising his left hand over his head as he flew under the checkered flag.

He lifted his foot for the safety lap as 27 blew past him, still flat out. As he coasted around the course now, the release of tension making him slightly giddy, he wondered vaguely just where he did finish. But it didn't matter now. He pulled off his helmet and enjoyed the icy feel of the wind where he had been sweating. Temperature and oil pressure seemed O.K. The clutch would get him home all right, but would need expensive work before it would race again.

He ran down the back straight at 75, the engine sounding smooth and confident. At the hairpin he noticed a small crowd forming around the damaged OSCAs.

"There are two boys with bigger bills than mine," he thought wryly. "They must have gone to fighting among themselves. I guess with one of those you've just *got* to be first. They wouldn't have done that on a safety lap so I suppose they didn't even finish. So old green must have won. And I had him until this bloody clutch started to go!"

"Hey, I'll have to do this again!"

14

Travels
with
Corvy

GRAN TURISMO" . . . ah! Grand Touring is a concept to stir the most jaded sophisticate. Breathes there a motorist with a soul so dead that he never to himself hath said, "Oh, for a *real* GT car, a big network of good roads, nothing between me and far horizons of delectation but a thin line of highway patrolmen, and plenty of time to enjoy it!" If such an opportunity drops suddenly into his lap, any car buff should literally jump for joy.

So it was with me. Howard was the fond proprietor of a new copy of America's only honest t'God GT car—the Corvette. We both had the time, and something resembling business, to make a 2,000-mile loop out into the Great West. And Howard was not only willing, but eager, to volunteer his jewel for the adventure. What delight! What a *nifty* notion!

Plans were laid, and the day, like Christmas, eventually arrived. There in the driveway, by dawn's early light, sat the gleaming white machine. It looked ferociously graceful, or gracefully ferocious, rather like a leopard. As I stuffed my gear behind the seat I was checked out by Howard on the essentials.

"She has the injected 350, not the big block. Better balance without all that weight up front. And still all the juice you can use. You'll see."

"Yeah, yeah!"

"To make up for the lack of inches, she has the four-eleven rear end. You can squeak her on any shift all the way out."

In view of those vast polyglass rollers on the rear wheels this was an impressive statement, but not, as it turned out, an exaggeration.

Feeling something between a kid in a candy store and a sultan returning to his harem after a long campaign, I slid behind the wheel. Very comfortable seat. Good back rake. Good pedal position. Good leg room, with the seat all the way back. One little thing, though. The wheel rim was about three inches from my diaphragm.

"Er, Howard, old man, how do you adjust the wheel? It seems to have been pulled all the way out."

"Sorry. That's where she stays. The drawing board guy had 16-inch arms."

"Oh. Well, yes. I see. Well. They say you can get used to hanging if you hang long enough. No problem."

(I have even learned to be comfortable at the wheel of a Volks bus. This gives me great—and in this case unwarranted—confidence in the structural adaptability of the human frame.)

With a bass rumble and words of cheer we rolled out and set forth. For the first miles we chugged along sedately, as road conditions dictated. "Just wait," I dreamed. "Pretty soon we'll be in the clear. Then we'll begin to live."

At low speeds it was evident that the car stuck tight to the road. Poured through close right angles it had imposing stability. Not surprisingly.

Shifting took a lot of muscle.

"Short throw, you know," said Howard. "Discourages much stirring around with the box, but you don't need to shift much."

This was true. The four-eleven gave us a high gear which seemed more like second, and it was hard to tell the four speeds apart without a program. So who needs a gear box? I soon learned to leave it pretty much alone.

Steering good. Brakes good. I lowered a window to adjust the side mirror. Loose, it flopped out of alignment as soon as we hit a bump. I made a note to tighten that at the first pit stop.

Naturally, the fuel gauge started precipitately down its arc. At the edge of civilization we were already below the middle mark, but since no station was open yet we headed blithely out across the prairie.

The sun was now well up.

"All the comforts of home," said Howard. "Shall we refrigerate?"

He flipped switches on the air conditioner. The cockpit filled rapidly up with smoke.

"Got a fire extinguisher?"

"Sure have."

"Let's go back anyway. That guy may be open by now."

He wasn't, but we got the hood up and, after some speculation, decided that the condenser in the conditioner had cooked itself.

"Can we replace that along the way?" I asked. "Parts of this route can be quite hot."

"'Fraid not. Big job. $350. No problem though—I can get parts at 50% off."

"That's nice."

Cheerfulness is essential on a long motor trip.

We opened the windows. The increased drag almost emptied the tank short of the next gas station, but we made it. Now, however, we were really out in the open. Flexing my synthetic muscles, I let the pedal down an inch.

Tilt.

Above 4,000 something didn't want to deliver. Power came off and on with fitful lunges.

"Am I doing something wrong?"

"Well, it's that I haven't been using the upper end since I tore off a fan belt at high revs. She seems to be out of tune. Probably the plugs."

"You tore off a fan belt?"

"Yeah. Almost fried the engine before I could exit the freeway. I think maybe the pulleys are out of alignment."

So. We had unhappy electricals. But this didn't matter because if we revved the engine we endangered the belts. We couldn't shift, much, but that didn't matter because we had a very low high. Besides, the shift knob, which was of metal rather than wood, was now too hot to touch. And then, of course, our air conditioning was out. Hmm. On the plus side, it was not far between gas stations. And she cornered like a dream, which would be nice if we made it across the prairie.

We pressed on—after breakfast (and 19 more gallons of premium). On the long rise approaching the mountains I inexcusably forgot myself and called for about 4,700, passing a farm truck. There was a snap and the heat gauge started up.

"That's it!" cried Howard (cheerfully). "Pull over on the shoulder."

Howard is a good amateur motor mechanic. He needs to be. In a very few minutes he had re-rigged the other belt so that we could make it back to the last town on the battery. We looked briefly for the broken belt, but assumed that it had been flung into the bushes along the verge. It hadn't.

Back in town we found a good parts house with a great array of belts and shortly we were road-worthy again. In a way.

In the interval we put in 16 more gallons of high test and I suggested to the man that he might tighten up the mirror.

"That kind you don't tighten," he said. "You throw them away and get new ones."

"Often?"

"Spring and fall."

So who needs a side mirror? If we can get along without speed, shifting, or air, we can bloody well do without a side mirror. Cheerfulness—that's the word.

For the rest of the first day things went swimmingly. We ground along from gas station to gas station at 3,500 rpm, while pickups and Volkswagens sailed by us on the outside. We knew she would steer, corner, and brake beautifully, should the occasion ever arise. And she ran real cool in the heat—the engine, that is, not the passengers.

I was glad to hand over to Howard. I find that a day's practice is not enough to make driving with your elbows at acute angles comfortable. By this time mine had taken a semi-permanent set.

The next day passed without incident, except when I tried to straddle a rock about the size of a lemon and found out about road clearance. This was a sore trial for Howard's cheerfulness, but he made a mighty effort. I grinned like Disney's Pluto and swore I'd never do it again.

As time and miles passed we became aware of certain fringe effects of Grand Touring in America's only true road machine. The gendarmerie regarded us with deepest suspicion and the peasantry with extravagant admiration; both, under the circumstances, without much justification. In the gas stations (and we came to know most of them) we were a sensation. Our approach to the pump resembled that of a victorious Roman general entering the sacred gates. We swaggered—in the pits if not on the circuit. A nice additional touch was that the engine would rarely stop when the ignition was cut, but would clank on threateningly, suggesting a lion unhappy in his cage. Heady stuff, marred only by dumb little kids who sneered when told we didn't have a 454.

On the fourth day we made a mistake. Our proposed route included 28 miles of dirt road, and, like fools, we followed it. Not that it was a bad dirt road—actually it was in very good shape—but I think that somewhere in the owner's manual one is told explicitly not to take a Corvette off the pavement, and *smooth* pavement at that. If not, the passage should be added. We made the 28 miles in a rousing hour and seventeen minutes, and Howard very nearly lost his cool. (Among other things, the injector had no air cleaner.)

O.K. No more dirt roads. O.K.

Now, in the green mountains, for a bit of top-downing. You know how the top panels and the rear window come out, leaving an open car with an airfoil roll bar? Very sexy.

Small point. The only place you can stow the top hamper is where you stow your suitcase. Hmm. I suggested we lash the gear on the gleaming chrome luggage rack gracing the poop deck. Howard nixed this.

"That rack is stuck onto the plastic body in a somewhat delicate manner, and besides the rack itself is made of *very* light tubing. Got to save weight, you know."

"Looks great, though. That waitress at breakfast really flipped over it. We don't want to spoil that effect by tying a lot of stuff all over it, do we?"

We remained friends.

It would have been too much to ask for a clean run home, even at a blistering 3,000 in whatever gear takes the place of high with a four-eleven. It was.

Conveniently at noon the cockpit began to fill again with black smoke. Smugly we knew it couldn't be the air conditioner. Still we had to push up our goggles and tilt one wing down, looking for a smooth pasture in which to land our Sopwith Camel, while shaking our fists at the Red Baron.

Everything in the engine room was smeared with oil and smoking, but there seemed to be no leak under the valve covers. On the hoist, the problem was discovered.

The vanished fan belt had wrapped around the propellor shaft and, in due course, had wrecked the front oil seal. Fortunately there was a Chevrolet agency in town. Fortunately they had a seal. (Howard explained that this was a conspicuous advantage of the 350 engine. He was sure we never could have found a seal for a big block. Very cheerful guy, Howard.) We persuaded the service manager, against all his training and judgment, to take on the job immediately. After two hours (most of which I spent drinking cold draft beer in an air-conditioned tavern nearby) we were ready to put in 20 more gallons and trundle on.

"Helluva note!" said Howard. "That seal only cost a buck sixty-five and they charged $28.50 just to put it on."

"Way it goes, nowadays." When confronted with frayed nerves, be banal. Try to be witty under these conditions and you invite blows to head and body.

No further beset, we wheeled her home. Apart from taking a couple of hours longer than planned to get from any point to any other point, it had been a good trip (oops!) voyage. When asked, we roundly praised the car's superb handling qualities, fierce acceleration, and cool-running engine. God's truth!

Believe me, "Grand Touring, American Style," is the only way to fly!

(If Howard happens to read this, I'm only kidding.)

15

Attention from the Left

THEY ARE NOT VERY SHARP. I arrived on a Friday and it took them until the following Thursday to discover who I was, what I was doing, and what they wanted to do about it. On the other hand, my hosts briefed me at once on the appearance, methods, and capabilities of the opposition. When the time arrived I was neither surprised nor completely unprepared.

That morning, as we approached the club where I had taught all week, their lookout was in position—the wrong position, if he did not intend to attract attention. His face, dress, bearing and actions were all wrong for the job. In a poor barrio, populated by Indians, he was clearly not an Indian. He was young and blond, with a short blond beard. He wore a white shirt, pressed trousers, and shoes. He smoked. All these things made him conspicuous.

There was no point in dissimulation. I stared right at him as we drove slowly by, and he met me with a flat, direct glare—the assassin's gaze, memorizing his target.

The day was normal, and we finished at six o'clock. After one beer I sent for the car and went out on the club house terrace. Pedro Izarra was with me.

A car turned in at the club gate. A late model U.S. sedan. One man driving. Two in the rear seat. Young. Neatly dressed. All according to briefing. CONDITION ORANGE.

"Watch it!" hissed Pedro. "This's the F.A.R."

"Got it. I've got it."

I didn't know quite what to do, but a big pistol, together with full competence in its use, is a great comfort. A big pistol, cocked and locked, rode on my hip, and teaching its use is my business. As they rolled up it was nice to know that they could do nothing to me that I couldn't do to them first. So I just stood there.

The car moved by us from right to left, made a U-turn and came back to stop just in front of the terrace. The two in back had slid forward off the seat but I could see their heads. The eyes of the three had never left us.

They had played it wrong, and they evidently realized it. They like to kill, but they don't like to fight. Possibly they did not realize their own peril, but possibly there was some sort of transmission of attitude. The range was about ten feet and at that distance I could take the two, enfiladed as they were, before they could bring their guns to bear. Pedro could take care of the driver, who probably was not planning to shoot anyway. Maybe they knew this and maybe not, but they are essentially cowardly and the scene did not appeal to them. Another time would be better.

The driver got out and came around the front. As he spoke to Pedro he kept his eyes on my face. His Spanish was terse, crude, "jivey." It does not translate well.

"You guys seen José Figueres?"

Pedro was so intent on the possibility of his forthcoming draw that he hardly moved his mouth as he answered.

"Is he a member of this club?"

"Yeah, man. He hangs around here a lot."

This youngster, too, was blond, but not the same man. No beard. Longish hair. The cigarette stuck to the lip in French fashion. Blue eyes.

I concentrated on the two in the back seat, though it was now very unlikely that they would start anything, with the driver out of the car.

"I haven't seen him," said Pedro.

"No? Well thanks, buddy."

"For nothing." The common Spanish locution seemed oddly appropriate.

The driver looked around for perhaps ten seconds, then got back in and spun his wheels on the gravel drive as he left. Irritable.

"Those were the boys, hey?" I asked Pedro.

"That they were. A lot of them around. They always try to find an easy way."

"Should we call the police?"

"You are very innocent. The man who answered the telephone could well be one of *them*. Besides, they didn't *do* anything."

True. They hadn't done anything. Perhaps we were just jumpy. It's a little hard to adjust one's thoughts to this sort of thing without practice. This is my only explanation for the fact that we did not shift over to a war footing that very night. But we didn't. A mistake.

Friday was uneventful. Saturday they tried again.

We left the club at 6:30 (such regularity is foolish) in Anselmo's car, a large American sedan. A light rain was falling, but it was not yet dark enough for headlights. As we passed the point where the lookout had been on Thursday morning, another out-of-character character watched us. Looking back (you get the habit of looking behind you in this country) I saw him turn and enter the side street. I think I saw him raise his arm as he disappeared.

No car had been following us as we left the club. Now, after a long ten-count, one came out of the sidestreet. U.S. made. Late model. Four doors. Dark color. Black or dark blue. Full of people—all men. ALERT.

Coincidence? Possibly, but this is a killing environment. *¡Cuidado!*

We make a left turn. The black car makes a left turn. Still, this is the regular route into town. We turn right. The black car follows, about two lengths back.

"Anselmo, hang a left at the light. I think we've got company." (This turn is *not* on the way to town.)

We turn. So does the black car.

"That's it!" says Anselmo, and produces his pistol. A 380. Not much of a pistol. Mine, now in my hand, is a Super 38. I would prefer my own 45 but that is a prohibited caliber in this country. (Big deal. Prohibited calibers.) In any case, the Super will have to do. Its trigger and sights could be a lot better, but its ten-round capacity and good penetration in car bodies are comforting. A man inside a car is no problem for a Super. There are at least six men in the black car. With an extra full magazine on my belt I have 19 rounds available. Used carefully, 19 should be plenty. Anselmo's 380 is almost useless, and Anselmo must also drive.

"What do we do?" I ask.

"We stay ahead. They always shoot from alongside."

So I have been told. They come up, preferably on the left, so that two machine pistols may be used at a range of four feet. Crude but workable. Now we must see that they can't bring it off. The streets are narrow and there is much evening traffic. Neither car can move rapidly. We proceed at the slow pace of a nightmare, the black car two lengths back.

We make numerous, meaningless turns. The black car follows. There is no longer any possibility of coincidence. And we know what they intend. It has been happening regularly for years. They may not be very skilfull, but they are *not* kidding. CONDITION RED.

I slide over into the back seat and roll down both windows. Glass adds a little to the resistance of a door, and I have more freedom to fire.

We are held up by a left turn. Now they could easily get out on both sides and open up, but the distance is too great for certainty with their limited skill, and also they fear identification. There is another thing, though they may not know it. I have been demonstrating with that Super for six days and I know where it shoots. The first man will die before he can fire. The others may get off some rounds, but they probably will be badly directed.

117

My feelings are confused. The first dismay at finding myself in harm's way has changed to intent worry. I *think* I can stay alive in this tactical situation, but what a mess! Police. Jails. Embarrassment. Friends compromised. Passports lifted. Publicity. A mess! And this brings on anger. These oafs! These impudent morons! Outrageous! Let's see how they look over the sights! Let's *have* it!

Now, as an artistic touch, Anselmo's car begins to falter. At throttle pressure it gasps. Out of gas? No. Carburetion.

"Come on—come ON!" he growls in agony of soul as the motor misses, catches, and misses again.

Fear? Yes, some. I feel no butterflies, nor does my hand shake, but my mouth is dry. I concentrate on the marksmanship problem. If either of their doors opens, beat them to the pavement—then *hold* and *squeeze.* Look at the sights, not the target. Shoot for the center of mass. Make every break a surprise break—every shot a ten . . .

Better yet—let's get away. Anselmo seems to have the engine under better control now and skilfully keeps thrusting the car into narrow openings where there is no room on either side. The pace remains slow, not at all as in the movies.

There's a break. We slip in front of a crossing truck and the black car cannot. We pass two small, rickety passenger cars, with our wheels up on the sidewalk, and the black car is further delayed. As soon as we think they might not be able to see it we turn and dodge up into a maze of side streets. We work across town and out onto the Reforma. No black car behind. We turn off, U-turn and wait, motor running. Nothing. We have lost them. Well.

We proceed in roundabout fashion back to the private home where I am staying, rapidly but not so fast as to attract the police, or those who appear to be police. The F.A.R. has a supply of police uniforms and you're never sure just who is behind a badge unless you know him personally.

We roll up and honk for the iron gate to be opened, joking perhaps a little too loudly for humor.

"Anselmo, amigo, I must really thank you for the most *interesting* ride home that I can remember. But one thing, please get yourself a bigger gun."

For the rest of my stay we moved in three-car convoys.

16

Nocturne
in the
Ten Ring

IT IS THE TIME OF RAINS in the land of coffee—a time when that land is so beautiful it hurts the eyes. The scene is emerald on jade, with flecks of topaz, ruby, and sapphire. Great thunderheads, white and grey, rumble across the soft blue sky and curl around tall volcanic cones that ring the valley. The air is clean and sweet and warm like a lover's breath. And overall lies fear—a steady, pervasive, ceaseless awareness of the imminence of sudden death.

This is the plantation of Elizaldo Pico, easier to measure in square miles than in acres. Its harvests travel yearly to all the tables of the free world, and bring back a measure of wealth sorely needed by an agricultural nation. The plantation provides work and income for thousands of subsistence farmers who live on it and know it as their land. The enemy wants it destroyed, so that production will cease, economy will fail, chaos and ruin will triumph, and "social justice" may be imposed at gunpoint.

The enemy concentration lies no more than three miles distant, by a good road. It is a town that has a pleasant sounding name on the map, but is known locally as Moscú. It elects a deputy regularly to the national legislature, whose function is to assure that it will not be bothered by the police or the national guard. It is supplied, administered, and directed from Havana.

It is dusk. Five men and three women sit around a broad table on the tiled terrace, with open bottles of an ambrosial West Indian rum perfuming the evening. Over the lawn beneath the canopy of a colossal ceiba, fireflies wink. They are lovely, but they suggest the distant flash of the assassin's rifle. There is a pistol on every man's belt, and there are carbines and shotguns by the chairs. There are riflemen out beyond the light. We believe they are all ours.

In the courtyard, one of the guards is softly singing "La Llorona." *La Llorona,* the weeper . . . the eerie Tehuana song about the ghostly woman who wails in the night wind. To hear her is to know of approaching death. To look her in her fleshless face is to die. The melody is plaintive and minor. La Llorona . . .

I am a gringo consultant employed by Don Elizaldo to advise him in matters concerning the defense of his operations, his property, his person, and his family. We have been working this afternoon out on the land, and we have made progress. The mood is genial.

"*¡Salud, y dinero—y tiempo para gastarlas!*" Wouldn't that be nice? Elizaldo Pico has a full share of the first two. It's the third that he may not have. Many of his friends have fallen to the enemy. Too many. He may last another year. Or more. Or tonight may be the night. He does not expect to die in bed. Still, he wants to make the enemy's job just as difficult as he can. He can't make it impossible, but he can make it extremely perilous. That is where I can help.

The dueño is in his middle prime—a cultivated, attractive, quiet man. His thin features, lightly greying hair, narrow reading glasses, and mild eyes suggest a professor of economics or of law. In fact Don Elizaldo does hold a law degree and is often addressed as "Licenciado." His somewhat pedantic appearance is further accentuated by a soft voice pitched rather higher than average and his habit of making notes on conversations he thinks important. It is a little startling to meet this professorial person in his normal working dress, with a 30 caliber paratroop carbine slung over his right shoulder and a 45 Commander at his left hip.

The evening deepens. The talk is cheerful. We speak of skin diving, of music, of our children. We do not discuss our day's work, or the fact that a neighbor who also wished my services will not be needing them now. He was killed last week.

La Llorona . . .

Children play around us, in the manner of Latin families. They are not loud or impudent, nor do they interrupt. "All children should be Latin American, at least to the age of fourteen," as the saying goes. The little girls have liquid eyes and pierced ears. The boys are leaving childhood and absorb the scene, fascinated by the company of warrior adults. The oldest son, already a good shot, obviously worships his father, the more because he knows as well as anyone that the remaining time of his company and counsel may be short. No generation gap here.

Doña Antonia, wife of the dueño, has the hardest destiny. Growing a bit plump, as is customary in this land, she is still an attractive and considerate hostess, fluent in four languages. She acts as if she were entertaining friends in Brentwood, but she knows. She prays for relief—for a day without fear—but her prayers, like those of millions of women since the dawn of man, will remain unanswered.

La Llorona . . .

I am to leave soon, but not according to any schedule or set time. In this way of life, regularity or routine is death. No orders are given, no dates are made, more than five minutes in advance of the act.

The ladies withdraw, and the conversation becomes more direct.

"You did very well today, my friend," I say. "Much improvement since the second day."

"Thank you. But I have a long way to go. It is difficult to change one's system completely in such a short time."

"Yet you understand why you should. You saw the results."

"Of course. There is no question about that. We will keep at it."

"If you do, you can reach about 80% of your capacity by harvest time. And that's when you will be most vulnerable."

This particular plantation has not had an "incident" in over a month, but since the initiative lies with the enemy, we cannot know when there will be another. Last year at this time twenty-five persons were murdered here in about 90 days. "It was more like a war then," says the dueño. "Every couple of days another body in the road. A battlefield."

The pressure is fairly constant throughout the land. The murders occur about equally on the plantations and in the capital, more often in daylight than by night. The favorite weapon is the machine pistol, inexpertly used. If the enemy were skilfull, the toll would be much higher. But he is not very efficient, nor very bright, and certainly not very brave. His strengths are persistence and savagery, together with his Cuban support and direction. The automatic weapons, the ammunition, the grenades are in lavish supply. At least they are for the enemy. The government, like most governments, is diligent in its efforts to disarm its decent citizens. There is registration, licensing, and confiscation. This, of course, has no effect at all upon the enemy, while it constitutes an expensive nuisance for those who try to abide by the law. To ask a man to be unarmed in this struggle is like sending a defenseless scout ship into hostile waters without air cover. Governments sometimes do both.

The police are infiltrated. A phone call for help may well be answered by one of *them* on the switchboard. And calls for help are too late in any case. These fights are over in seconds, one way or another. My task is to see that they end in our favor.

"You understand that these people are utterly without principle," continues Elizaldo Pico. "A sign of the times, I suppose. A degeneration of morals that is apparent in your country, too. I am not a soldier, but I think that in some wars it is possible to feel a certain respect for one's enemies. That is not true here. Here they show only treachery and cowardice. It is not possible to respect them. Yet they do kill."

"And you kill them, too."

"Sometimes. With luck. But not as often as it will take to end this thing. To do that, we must have the army. 'Search and destroy' as you do in Viet Nam. But the government will not do that, because that is to admit that we are at war. That is 'escalation,' as you put it so quaintly. So it goes on."

"You could pack up and leave. You don't exactly need a job."

A wintry smile.

"I will not leave. Nor my wife, nor my children. I bought this finca two years ago from one they scared away. Now it is my land and this is my country. I will not be driven from it by these mindless brutes. This is a fine country—a beautiful land, rich and productive. It can have a wonderful future, but not if it is given over to lunatics whose one solution to any argument is murder. No, I will not leave. Do you think I ask your help in order to leave?"

"No, señor. The point was clearly academic. Yet you do show admirable steadfastness and dignity in your position. In formal wars men are bound by orders. You have no orders, yet you commit yourself to an indefinite tour of duty. That is courage."

"It may be. But you have fought in various wars. You should know. I will take your word for it."

"I've never fought in one like this, though. This one is weird. It's not a cataclysm like those I lived through as a youth, but it is still not pretty."

More than ever like a professor, the dueño speaks slowly and clearly that I may understand his Spanish.

"In the twentieth century we have had three classes of wars, all total. First we had the static war of great empires, an essentially defensive war ruled by the technology of the time. This was World War I.

"Then we had the mobile war of national ideologies, in which you served. Its fluidity was likewise dictated by the march of technology. This was World War II.

"And now we have World War III, the war of international ideologies. It's all one war, whether fought in Korea, or Viet Nam, or along the Sino-Indian frontier, or in the streets and on the campuses of your country, or here on my farm. In this one war there are many fronts and many battles. Right here, right now, I do my small best to help us all. As do you."

"You make me ashamed to take your check, señor."

"No, no, no. You must not be. It is your profession, and you should be properly compensated. Your government paid you to fight, did it not? And I realize a profit (or hope to, with God's help) on my coffee. This is incidental. What is important is not that one is paid, but that one risks his life for what he thinks is right. You would not work for *them*, at any wage. Do not feel that you are an employee here. You are our friend and guest."

"That's very kind, patrón. I can only hope and pray that our work together has truly helped."

"But it has. Already it has. In confidence alone, we feel stronger, safer."

"Well that in itself is quite a lot. Let's hope you don't have to use what I have taught you, but, if you do, let us pray that you will take full advantage of it."

Again the cold smile. Elizaldo Pico looks out at the velvet night, sparkling with elfin light, then turns and stares at a crude banner that was tacked up over an unguarded storehouse two nights ago. *"Viva la Revolución Cubana!"* it says, *"Viva la F.A.R."* (The storm troops of the enemy call themselves the *Fuerza Armada Rebelde.*) The banner he now displays like a trophy.

"We will use it, maestro, never doubt. *Ojalá* that we use it well."

"I hope you will not take it as idle bluster if I say that I would like to be at your side when the time comes."

"I know you mean what you say, and it would indeed be a comfort, but there is no need. You have your work to do, as I have mine. If you can work with as many others as possible you will be doing more for what we both believe in than you could with one gun, no matter how well you use it."

The guard in the courtyard has finished his song, but the sound persists in the mind. Life and death seem more intimately interwoven than usual in this rich tropic night. We have perspective. We know what is important and what is not. We are brothers. *Muy emocionante.*

The time for parting has come, decided on the instant. Orders are given. The ladies re-appear for farewells.

Muy agradecido, señora. Muy amable.

A man with a Thompson follows Elizaldo Pico as he steps inside the radio room, his command post.

"Attention, the main gate! In ten minutes hit the lights and open up. There will be three cars. Acknowledge. Over."

As with a naval party entering boats, everyone takes his seat before the principal. The motors are running. I exchange handshake and abrazo with the dueño. I resist the tendency to salute. It would not be "correct," but I've never felt an occasion more appropriate.

Adios.

I get in the car. Starboard side aft. Both windows down. The best shooting position. I am supposed to be the best shot. I don't check my sidearm. A man who is not sure of the condition of his weapon at all times has no business in this business.

Elizaldo Pico, standing back out of the courtyard light, flicks a signal with his flashlight to the first car. It moves. To our car. We move. And to the car behind. As the convoy rolls out I look back to see the scholar walking again toward the radio room, carbine black down his right side, machine-gunner in attendance.

The fireflies wink. The cars accelerate. We go through the gate at fifty miles an hour, twenty-five yards apart. We reach the highway and head back to the capital, a small blue light behind each windshield telling us that the following car is ours, not theirs.

The engine hums. The seat is comfortable, as is the feel of the heavy pistol I have slid out of its holster and placed under my right thigh. It has been a full day.

As we glide along, my companion starts to sing. The melody has stuck in his mind, too.

La Llorona . . .

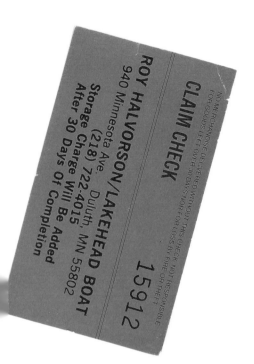

CLAIM CHECK
ROY HALVORSON/LAKEHEAD BOAT
940 Minnesota Ave.
(218) 722-4015
Duluth, MN 55802
Storage Charge Will Be Added
After 30 Days Of Completion
NO MERCHANDISE DELIVERED WITHOUT THIS CHECK NOT RESPONSIBLE
FOR GOODS LEFT OVER 30 DAYS NOR FOR LOSS BY FIRE OR THEFT
15912

17

Mental Conditioning for Combat

Mortal Combat is a startling experience. Even those who engage in it quite frequently don't really get used to it, and very few people are ready the first time. This is especially true of the junior police officer, who, no matter how well he has been trained, finds that looking up his first gun barrel is something he can hardly believe. It happens so suddenly. There you are, on routine duty as always, somewhat bored and looking forward to getting off watch, and then in an instant you are a split second away from death. If you do everything right you will survive. If you don't—well, you still may survive (goblins are usually bad shots), but only by the grace of God. Adjusting one's mind to these conditions takes a bit of doing.

One's personal defensive weapons may be good or bad, and one's skill in their use may vary from splendid to spastic, but neither a fine gun nor prize-winning marksmanship matter if they are not used. The decision to use them must come from a properly conditioned mind, and it must come immediately. This is hard. A normal human being is not programmed to kill without emotional preparation. Therefore a man who is equipped and trained to use lethal violence must "pre-set" himself to respond in a certain way to certain kinds of stimuli, according to hypothetical decisions made in advance and "fed into his computer."

125

In a classic case a couple of years ago a young officer in a two-man patrol car made a man-with-gun stop on the highway. As his partner commenced arrest procedures, the young man got out on his side of the car and stood ready, with his shotgun at high-port. He stood there and watched as the felon in the halted car opened the door and shot him in the chest with a 357. He was certainly well armed, he certainly could have hit at an estimated range of 20 feet, and he had ample time, but he died in amazement, without firing a shot. His mind had not been pre-set for the possibility which killed him.

On another recent occasion a police officer answering a "shooting-in-progress" call was hit in the spleen with a 22, *after both he and the felon had emptied their weapons and reloaded.* He got off his six rounds all right, but he shot from belt level, a totally inappropriate stance for the distance involved. He reacted, but incorrectly. One deliberate squeeze could have saved his life (he was a good shot), but he tripped the wrong mental switch and he died as a result.

And what shall we say of the commonplace shootings of police officers *with their own guns?* Clearly a man who has his pistol taken from him is in an entirely unsuitable state of mind at the time. You can't snitch a man's gun if he expects you to try. Any man—soldier, policeman, or private citizen—who wears a sidearm must bear constantly in mind that not everyone within arm's length is necessarily his friend.

We need not belabor the obvious truth that when one carries weapons he assumes a grave social responsibility. Shooting a man is a very serious matter, justified only in dire circumstances, and when we carry a pistol we are bound to give the matter our deepest thought. The legal aspects of shooting are a study in themselves, but there are moral and emotional facets of the subject that stand outside the law.

First let's consider the ubiquitous question about "shooting to kill." The use of this phrase marks the user as one unfamiliar with firearms in general and with defensive pistolcraft in particular, but it is common enough with journalists and some legalists. The fact is that it is, as most commonly heard, meaningless. The only adequate reason for shooting a man is to prevent his doing something awful. Usually that will be his killing you, though it can be his killing someone else, or the activation of an explosive or incendiary device. It can also be to prevent his escape, providing that you are convinced beyond any doubt, and prepared to prove it before God and the law, that he certainly will do something awful if he does get away.

Thus we are never much concerned with killing, but we are vitally concerned with *stopping. If we shoot at all, we shoot to stop.* Nineteen times in twenty this means that we shoot for the center of mass. In the twentieth case we shoot for the brain. In no case do we shoot to disable—simply because we aren't that good. Defensive combat is split-second work. Some of us, it is true, can hit a man in the elbow in a split second at short range—much of the time. But not always—under pressure, under fire, in motion, in dim light. No marksman in the world is so good that he can shoot to wound and be absolutely sure that he will not kill—not under combat conditions. Therefore, we must conclude that if an adversary needs shooting, he needs killing. If he doesn't, we are not justified in the use of the gun.

Question: "Did you shoot to kill?"

Answer: "No, sir. I shot to stop."

The next point involves what some moralists call "playing God." We hear the query, "But do I *ever* have the moral right to decide that a man shall die by my hand? Shouldn't that be up to the courts? Doesn't scripture say, 'Thou Shalt Not Kill!'?"

Very well. Let's consider the Commandment. In the King James Bible, and many other English language translations, the word "kill" is unqualified. This is an error. In the original Hebrew the word used connotes *unjustified* killing—murder. The Old Testament specifically authorizes taking human life justly ("Thou Shalt Not Suffer a Thief to Live!" Deut: 24:10) and scripture tells us of any number of powerful, and moral, fighters, from Little David on down. Killing, for a good and proper reason, is a perfectly acceptable act—to most of us. A man who does not think so should not be a cop, nor should he bear arms in any capacity. The problem, of course, comes to a head in the case of the man who feels that while socially directed killing may be moral, he, himself, is not justified in making that decision personally on the spot. This is possibly a valid attitude for a private citizen, but not for a policeman. The policeman is a sworn protector of society, and he must be prepared to make the lethal decision, under conditions dictated by law and his conscience.

It really isn't all that hard—most of the time. In that notable photo taken in 1973 on a California parking lot we see a goblin sitting on a girl he has wrestled to the ground, the point of his knife in her throat. Behind him is a security guard, his 45 locked in, two-handed, on the murderer's head. An instant after the picture was taken he fired, we are told. The girl escaped with a scratch, though the experience was one that may well affect her emotionally for a long time. This may have been "playing God," but I can't see it as presumptuous in this case.

On another occasion in Connecticut a counter-culture type, possibly crazed by drugs, took it upon himself to disembowel his pregnant cohabitress with a butcher knife, right on the sidewalk. The police car arrived too late to save the girl's life, but caught the man horribly and literally red-handed, still chopping at his mangled victim. Even for a veteran cop this was a frightful sight. As the monster (no, I won't call him a "suspect") turned and ran, the policeman drew and called upon him to stop—or so he says. (Many of us do not much care whether he did or not.) At that point the policeman made a decision, and fired, catching his target low and center in the head, and thereby saved the community a great deal of time, trouble, and money. I cannot see any cause for remorse on this policeman's part.

These things happen. We must be aware of that. We need not worry about taking too much upon ourselves in making decisions in such cases, because, for the most part, the decision will be obvious. If it is not, we don't fire. Simple.

FireWorks

If a man is about to kill us, we fire. If he is about to kill an innocent party, we fire. If he is an atrocious felon, ready to commit another atrocity if he escapes, we fire. These decisions are not hard to make—at leisure. What is necessary is to prepare to make them instantly.

The lethal decision must, of course, really be a conscious decision, not a conditioned reflex. This demands a clear, quick mind that not everyone can claim. But by analyzing and anticipating the problem we can prepare our minds to handle a hypothetical question faster. We can employ the venerable mental exercise of the junior officer—"What will I do if . . . ?" In situation after situation, both imaginary and real, we can ask ourselves that question. Then, when a real tactical decision is called for, we will be prepared.

Elaborate training aids exist to sharpen our combat wits. They can be expensive and are not always available to everyone, but they are both interesting and useful. One of the best is a cinema booth in which a live situation is vividly represented in both color and sound. The student is "read into the problem" by a voice track, and enters the booth armed with a weapon that will stop the scene and record his hit, if he chooses to fire. As a "guinea pig" on such a device, I remember that my response to the briefing was that if I saw a gun barrel pointed in my direction I would fire. (The briefing postulated no other lawman on the scene.) The scenario was pretty exciting, and included some highly provoking action, but, while I drew and went to the Weaver Ready position, I did not fire until I saw that gun. The machine logged a center hit in .65 seconds—on the right man. I do not recount this as a boast, but only to illustrate how a pre-set decision can be made to work. It is obvious that working with a machine is a far cry from a live gunfight, but, once we have accepted the proper philosophy about the justified use of deadly force, the difference is not great enough to invalidate our preparations.

I have now been conducting training in modern defensive pistolcraft for over a decade, and one thing that has become very clear is that sheer marksmanship is not enough. Some students turn out to be better shots than others, of course, but becoming a good, fast shot is only the first half of the exercise. To prepare the second half I have devised a simple color code which is used to enable the student to assume a state of mind appropriate to the various stages of readiness he may need. A man cannot live constantly looking down his sights with his finger on the trigger. As you read this, for example, you are not emotionally prepared to shoot at a living enemy. But you can, with a bit of practice, learn to switch your mind into a more advanced state of readiness, in which certain pre-set decisions are easier to make. You do this naturally, but usually by an infinitely variable gradation. The color code makes it easier, by means of definite, pre-considered steps. It works thus:

"Condition White" is a normal, non-combative state of mind. It is where we would prefer to live. In Condition White we do not expect trouble. No one nearby constitutes any conceivable threat. We need not look behind us. We feel perfectly safe (with what we believe to be sufficient reason), and we are not armed. If we are attacked when in Condition White we will be completely surprised, and we will probably die.

128

"Condition Yellow" is a state of relaxed alertness. It must always be assumed whenever we wear a gun. In Condition Yellow we do not expect any specific hostile act, but we are aware that something of the sort is possible. We maintain an easy but steady 360° surveillance. We know who is behind us. We stay out of arm's length of strangers, insofar as possible. The policeman, on duty, is always on Yellow—except when he is on Orange or Red. A man can maintain Condition Yellow indefinitely, without undue nervous strain. He is not completely safe, but he is much safer than on White.

"Condition Orange" is a state of alarm. In Orange we have reason to believe that a fight is likely. We have a specific tactical situation in mind, and we have considered the provocations that may arise to justify our use of deadly force. We are careful to avoid "over-reaction" but we are thinking combatively. We keep our backs well covered. We cannot be surprised. A man cannot maintain Orange for very long, as his concentration must be completely devoted to the matter at hand. The pistol is holstered, if the subject is competent, but a carefully controlled shot is available in about three seconds' notice.

"Condition Red" is that of defensive combat. In Condition Red, if you see a deadly threat you shoot. You have made up your mind that that is what the situation warrants, and only certain pre-set checks (a badge, a uniform, etc.) will inhibit your fighting stroke. "All systems are GO." Your pistol may be holstered, but more often it will be in hand, and in either case a controlled shot is available in about one second. A policeman usually enters a tactical situation on Orange, and shifts to Red when he is shot at.

This color code is not advanced as the complete answer, or even the best answer, to mental preparation, but it has been very well received by my classes. It is difficult to assess its tactical application, for it applies mainly to circumstances prior to actual combat, but we can certainly see numerous cases wherein its absence proved disastrous. In the two instances cited, for example, the young man with the shotgun was on Yellow (or possibly even White) when he should have been on Orange. I cannot really say what the mental condition of the PPC (belt level) shooter was, except that it was *not* Red, as it should have been, since he was obviously playing, not fighting.

One of the surprising things about the color code is the degree of peace of mind it affords. Having thought the matter through, and thus prepared your alternatives in advance, you can discard your nervousness about how you are going to react when the whistle blows. It really does wonders for the pre-combat jitters. In so doing, it provides a large head start toward achieving the absolute essence of success in combat, which, to no one's surprise, is *coolness.*

To keep your cool when you have every reason not to is the mark of a man. It is in no sense an unattainable goal. The plaint I often hear, "But how do you expect me to keep my head when some goon is trying to kill me?," is unworthy of our serious consideration. We know you can do so because people have done so—not just once in a while but continuously throughout history. To find yourself suddenly in a situation that is exciting, unexpected, and terrifying is a sound test of your character. Pass it.

Keep cool, concentrate on your front sight and press smoothly, disregarding your enemy's fire. It can be done. Perfectly ordinary people do it all the time.

Deplore it as we may, personal, mortal combat is a very ordinary thing in our culture, and nothing suggests that this is going to change. To a large degree it is an attribute of a free society, for crime is easily stamped out by tyranny. The policeman opts for strife when he takes his job, and it would appear that a cop who is dismayed by violence is clearly in the wrong profession. Moreover, the private citizen must also face up to the probabilities of his cultural environment, and, unless he lives on a farm or in a slave state, these include fighting.

Winning a fight is nothing to be ashamed of, though there are indeed some complex souls who might have us think so. Killing a man who is trying to kill you, or who makes a business of preying upon the innocent, should be a source of pride—not a badge of shame. I know a man who has been employed in one of our biggest police departments for many years on its reaction squad. He and his colleagues respond to lethal violence with lethal violence, and they do it very well. I will not give his score here because I'm not sure of it as I write, but it was high when I last talked to him and it has doubtless grown since. Some would have you believe that this man must live a life of unimaginable nightmares, with all those killings on his conscience. Such is simply not the case. My friend is one of the most well-adjusted, open-hearted, uncomplicated, cheerful men I have ever met. His marriage is conspicuously happy, and his children are outstanding. He has no hang-ups, that anyone can tell. His business is blowing away bad guys, and it obviously relieves him of all his frustrations. We could use more like him.

So set your mind at ease. If you must fight, take the moral course and do your best. The obvious confidence that you can do it—that you are technically equipped, properly trained, and emotionally prepared—may well serve to abort a fight before it starts. This is not uncommon. But if things do come to a conclusion in "unmitigated act," a proper balance of physical and mental preparation will stack the deck heavily in your favor.

18

"We Have To Disarm the Citizens of This Country . . ."

Is THIS NEBUCHADNEZZAR speaking of Judea? Or William the Conqueror speaking of Saxon Britain? Or Cromwell speaking of Ireland? Or Kosygin speaking of Czechoslovakia?

No. This is Patrick V. Murphy, police commissioner of New York City, speaking of the United States of America.

In the name of George Washington, who in blazes is "WE," to presume to do anything to the citizens of the United States! The citizens of this country do unto themselves, Commissioner. They are not peasants to be disarmed by some bureaucratic cossack. Go read your history, Commissioner; or better, leave this country and go somewhere where your views are already honored and the citizens are already disarmed. The U.S.S.R., for example.

"Disarmed." That's the word. Taken aback, defeated, helpless, gelded, stopped. Not citizens then, but serfs. I do not exaggerate—that's what a serf was, disarmed. The man who attempts, plans, or even wishes to disarm me must be regarded as my mortal enemy. We have met such people overseas. It is sickening to find them not only in our midst, but in positions of influence.

"We must disarm the citizens of this country." That statement could only come from a declared enemy of this country. That statement is TREASON.

I cannot speak for all the citizens of this country, Commissioner, but I, for one, will not be disarmed. Not while I live. Mark that well.

19

What Is "Accuracy"?

TOWNSEND WHELEN—may he sit at the right hand of God—wrote, "Only *accurate* rifles are interesting." And it came to pass that the riflemen of the world heard and replied. "Yea, verily," and they caused to be propounded a dictum, to wit: "If it won't put 'em in the same hole, it ain't worth a damn."

Santayana defined a fanatic as one who redoubles his efforts after he has lost sight of his goals. Whelen was no fanatic, but his words have inspired a sort of fanaticism. This is no bad thing *per se*, but I think it can stand a bit of examination.

Shrinking group size is a worthy aim, but it is only part of the successful management of small arms—rifle or pistol. Pinpoint mechanical precision, measured in seconds of the angle, or even in full minutes, is interesting but not the primary object of the exercise. If one hole in a piece of paper is the entire purpose of marksmanship, anyone can achieve it simply by shooting only once. *Intrinsic* accuracy, in rifle or pistol, is a good thing, but it must be thought of as just one element of *practical* accuracy. Intrinsic accuracy that is beyond the capacity of the marksman to utilize, except possibly from a bench rest, is of little use except in a bench match. Now bench matches are fine, and they tell us much about the construction of firearms, but they relate to marksmanship rather as drag racing relates to Grand Prix. There is certainly a connection, but the one is only part of the other, larger, concept.

FireWorks

I am constantly asked about "accuracy jobs" on auto pistols. What kind, who does it best, and for how much? I try to respond gently by asking if the enquirer is sure he needs one. Unless he is a very fine shot he won't be able to tell a ten-minute pistol from a five-minute pistol, so why should he bother at all until his skill can justify the trouble?

Intrinsic accuracy is a function of barrel, chamber, lock-up, and ammunition. It has nothing to do with trigger, sights, form, or firing position. It is best tested in a machine rest (with certain odd exceptions). *Practical* accuracy, on the other hand, is the measure of what the shooter can do with the weapon, and, while it is thus a subjective consideration, skilled marksmen can still provide a reasonably uniform evaluation of it as applied to any given instrumental combination. (Obviously anyone who thinks a telescope sight will make his rifle "more accurate" has a bad case of semantic indigestion.)

Close examination of the relationship between intrinsic and practical accuracy has indicated that, given a useful if not excessive degree of the former, the latter is overwhelmingly more significant.

For example, I own a *Sturmgewehr* that really will keep its shots in ¾" at 100 yards—from a machine rest. It has coarse iron sights and a typical five-and-ten-cent-store trigger—if rather better than some of that sort. I also own a light hunting carbine taking the same cartridge. It *may* stay in two inches, on a good day, but I will not bet on it. It features a crisp, sharp scope and a crisp, sharp trigger. Which is "better"? Clearly we can't answer that, but if I had to grab one gun and run I would not hesitate. One piece provides superb intrinsic accuracy that I cannot use, the other affords just fair intrinsic accuracy that I *can* use. Naturally I would prefer the carbine to "put 'em in one hole" but it wouldn't really matter, because under field conditions—time pressure, heartbeat, wind, estimated range, variable light, improvised shooting stance, nerves—I can only shoot so well, and my personal control is measured here in full inches, not fractions thereof.

Consider this matter of group size. A two-inch, 100-yard group establishes that the combination under consideration (weapon, sights, ammunition, marksman, firing position, and time limit) can absolutely guarantee a hit *within one inch* of the exact point of aim. Most shots will be even closer than that, since two inches is the outside limit of the group. That is with a pedestrian two-inch gun. With a gilt-edge, one-inch gun we could cut that maximum divergence to one-half inch. At 100 yards we cannot even see increments so small, much less hold to them.

This is by no means to say that accuracy doesn't matter, because it certainly does. But it would seem that we have been conditioned overlong to the belief that small improvements in intrinsic accuracy can compensate for large deficiencies in marksmanship, and that notion is clear off the paper. An unimpressive rifle (three minutes, off a bench) can do a good job, in the hands of a good shot. But the most accurate rifle in the world is no better (and no worse) than a Tower Musket, in the hands of a bad shot. Can a good shot do better with a more accurate rifle? Yes, a little. Can a bad shot do better with one? No.

It is not a matter of absolutes, of course. There are degrees of intrinsic accuracy, as there are degrees of marksmanship. It is just that one degree of personal marksmanship is about fifty times more important than one degree of machine rest accuracy.

The measured firing stages for rifles at my range now vary from 25 to 1,000 meters. We see a lot of shooters, using many combinations of cartridges, weapons, sights, and positions. Hardly any one ever shows up who is not a great marksman—by his own testimony. Apparently nobody in Arizona has a rifle that won't print one-holers at 100 (present company excepted), but when we put the matter to a test something always turns up to spoil the show. I think what happens is that we have a strong tendency to speak of what happened once as what should be expected every time—just like airline schedules. This is perfectly understandable, but it does make for confusion. Any man who has shot a lot can remember some pretty remarkable feats, but we must bear in mind that it is what we can do "on demand," not what we may have done upon occasion, that matters. Unfortunately we rarely do bear this in mind, and consequently we often sound very foolish indeed.

There is a legend that almost any Boer farm lad (back in the days when boys were men and men were better) could hit an opponent in the head at 300 meters—four times out of five. (Never mind the conditions, which don't really matter, but we can assume a 7x57 G.I. Mauser, using issue sights, fired from prone.) Today's hotshots nod over this and comment that that was "pretty good," considering the primitive equipment available at the time. One might assume that they could do better given the range, the target, and the time. The thing is, I *have* the range, and the target, and the time. I can sing out, "Show me! Show me *now.*" No practice. No warm up. No sighting shots. Just do it.

You'd be surprised—or maybe you wouldn't—at the results.

Now all this is not to deride the splendid Boer tradition of marksmanship, nor even to embarrass today's thoughtless braggarts; but it does indeed raise serious questions about the value of accuracy that is beyond the reach of the marksman.

When the 264 was first introduced we ran across a party of hunters in the Kaibab, all proudly bearing the new and much admired "magnums." One of these heroes told me seriously at a Kaibab breakfast (a large but thin slice of ham, topped with two lightly seared slices of fresh deer liver, topped by two fried eggs) that the great new 264 would do at 400 yards what a 270 would do at 300. I was much impressed. These guys who can ice mule deer at three and four hundred yards must be very good indeed. Later on I saw that same hunter twice miss a buck cleanly at 120 steps, shooting over the hood of the Jeep, and again miss at 104 paces, offhand, by four or five feet.

The 264 is indeed a fine cartridge—both accurate and powerful. Perhaps it is better than the 270. It may even be "more accurate"—in some combinations. *But unless you can shoot up to it, who cares?*

What the man can't do, the rifle can't either.

Sometimes I think that we Americans are "equipment happy," believing that gadgetry is a good and proper substitute for skill. "Out where ranges are long, you need (here substitute your favorite brand name) performance." Balderdash. Out where ranges are long you need to know how to shoot. Led on by a fatuous belief that any man is automatically as good as any other, and that if he buys the right brand of goo he will automatically inspire unheard of concupiscence in all nubile females, we then naturally fall into the belief that if we don't shoot very well we can make ourselves do better by demanding more "accuracy" from our weapons. Well, some can. Very few, in my opinion. If we discard the consideration of out-and-out junk, perhaps one rifleman in fifty can shoot up to his weapon—one pistolman in a thousand. Let us by all means continue to pursue the excellent goals of Colonel Whelen, but let us not forget that it is the man, not the gun, that places the shot where it belongs.

20

Ballistic
Wampum

Economic sophisticates are no strangers to the notion that money, which all would like to think of as a conceptual reality, is actually an abstraction. Even, perhaps especially, the learned sages who convene now and again to consider and debate this arcane subject cannot satisfactorily define money. At a recent conference one member, in desperation, declaimed, "If the dog eats it, it's dog food!" Thus, if you can buy stuff with it, it's money. O.K. But this leaves us totally dependent upon the whim of the seller, does it not? He will accept what you offer him as money only as long as he has reason to believe that other people will accept it at the same value when *he* offers it to *them*—unless he can put whatever it is to his own personal use. The latter option is barter—chickens for legal advice, manual labor for food, et cetera.

As long as money is minted gold or silver, even though we cannot eat it, we have something other than good faith on which to base our prospects. Gold, particularly, is dependable in value under almost all conditions. A *trustworthy* entity (king, nation, company, bank) which promises to redeem its paper in gold, on demand, can issue pretty good money. Obviously when an *untrustworthy* entity does *not* so promise, what it issues as "money" has no value at all apart from a sort of social momentum.

As long as the United States held to the gold standard, and before expediency was placed above truth by Roosevelt II, U.S. paper money was a great thing to own—and spend. Now look at it. Would that more people would stop whimpering "Prices are going up," when what they mean is "The dollar is going down!" Why shouldn't it? It has *no* value other than what the fiscal libertines of the left say it has, and *they* have a license to print it without promising to redeem it for *anything*—not even peanuts. (I try to keep my sanity by thinking of dollars as dimes—earned, spent, or taxed. Whether that expedient has worked is moot.)

For the moment we try to get along by working feverishly for the dwindling paper dollar, because we have no choice. We don't know what the future holds, but we do know that we had better turn our cash into things while we still can. As matters are progressing now, that green stuff is heading toward the time when it will be useful mainly for starting fires.

(Fritz Hayek, one of the few significant modern economists, has now reached the conclusion that the only hope remaining is the termination of the government money monopoly and the institution of private minting. A stimulating theory, but don't hold your breath.)

All the foregoing is common knowledge, and those few who are both wise and fortunate—or wise and able—have been doing what they could to strengthen their economic dikes. However, as I scan what might be called "The Doomsday Press" I note that one obvious commodity is conspicuously lacking from the lists of what the wise should stock against disaster. This is ammunition. I do not mean ammunition as fodder for defensive and alimentary purposes, but ammunition as economic tender. In times of monetary collapse, ammunition (in a free, or recently free, country) is not only more valuable than any piece of paper, it is even more valuable than minted coin—*because you can use it.* You can't drink paper, and you can't eat gold (as the Araucanians forcibly demonstrated to the conquistador), but ammunition you can shoot, and by shooting you can both stock your larder and keep the ill-disposed off your back. Additionally and importantly, ammunition is neatly negotiable, being compact, accurately divisible, almost non-degenerative, and not as specialized as one might at first assume. One round of 22 long rifle is now worth about 3½¢. The moment you can't find it on the store shelf it is worth a nickel. After it has been unobtainable for three months it will get you a cup of ersatz coffee. And the minute The Revolutionary Committee for Public Order takes over and bans it, it will buy you a good breakfast.

Now, therefore, whenever I buy ammunition I buy two portions—"one for me and one for my friend." My friend, in this case, is a storage locker—tough, portable, and containing, in addition to its primary load, a package of "silica gel" or calcium carbonate as a dehumidifier.

Clearly the 22 long rifle is the big item. Everybody has a 22. The high-speed hollow-point is the best variety—it sounds better in a deal. I don't think you can have too much, but don't run out and buy a vast quantity. Big Brother is watching you.

For pistols, stock 38 Special, 357, and 45 ACP. Some Parabellum if you live in the East. And a couple of boxes of 380 and 32 ACP. These last may be essentially worthless but there are a good many pieces around to take them. In the West we want a bit of 45 Colt and 44 Magnum as well.

For rifles, the basic caliber is 308, closely followed by 30-06, 270, and 30-30. While 223 is increasingly popular with serious shooting types, such people probably have an adequate supply on hand and will not be beating the bushes in your direction. We have such a plethora of rifle calibers that no one could possibly stock them all, but you might look in on your local friendly gunstore (small type) and see what is on the shelf. He caters to the one-box-a-year man, and if that man owns an old 30-40 or 348 Winchester he will be hurting when the shelf goes bare.

For shotguns 12 and 20 will do, better standard length than magnum, loaded with number six birdshot. A few 410's may not be wasted. Here again you may have reason to stock specialties if you deduce the demand.

When (as we devoutly hope it won't) push comes to shove, you can start pistol rounds at 50¢ each (as of 10 February 1978) and rifle at $1.00. If history is any guide, when that time comes everything will immediately be declared illegal. *Everything*, from gasoline engines to criticizing The Committee. Guns of any kind, of course. But The Committee, or whatever it calls itself, will be even more illegal in the eyes of us mossbacks, and we will either come to some sort of modus vivendi or we will not. If we don't survive, we will have no worries about money, or anything else. If we *do*, our ammunition stocks will be our staff of life.

21

Rainbow's
End

SOME ORGANISMS SEEM PROGRAMMED to destroy their hosts. They are the unsuccessful parasites—smallpox, domestic sheep, the strangler fig; as opposed to the successful parasites—athlete's foot, lions, mistletoe. The human race must certainly be included in the first category, as we watch the accelerating corruption of our lovely planet by the breeding of billions of our own kind.

For dreaming ages the sparkling waters, the shadowed forests, the sculptured canyons, the mounded hills, the cleanly deserts, and the fragrant seas of grass lay pure and beautiful beneath a pristine sky. Life was begotten, born, fulfilled, evolved and destroyed, but its self-regulating balance left the earth uncorrupted. From the Pleistocene until just yesterday, the stage remained the same, simultaneously bountiful and harsh, beautiful and terrible.

The earth was not inimical to man, and it was apparently inexhaustible as his habitat. From the dim beginnings of civilization until a few generations ago, the wonder remained constant and magnificent. Tahiti, Capri, Kashmir, the Ohio, the Rhine, Jackson Hole, the Valley of Mexico, Ruwenzori, Laguna—these places did not change. They were there, century upon century, and that was enough.

But man *is* inimical to the earth. It took him six thousand years or more to get started, but now he is fully underway, and if he does not deliberately destroy himself first he will utterly befoul his nest and drown in his own waste. That mushroom cloud may be more benign than we imagine.

For those of us who take delight in the world as it was made, the boundaries ever more perniciously set by man's hate and envy inexorably shut off our ability to appreciate it. Only one hundred years ago any decent man, good natured and well provided, could go almost anywhere on the face of God's earth, doing proper homage to its creator by acknowledging its grandeur. There were a few places off limits, but they were mere specks of annoyance on the great canvass of adventure.

Today, by contrast, those who cherish the wilderland know that most of what is not forbidden is polluted, and as fast as exceptions are discovered they are overrun, ravished, and consumed.

As a boy, some fifty years ago, I read this:

> " 'I speak of Africa and golden joys'; the joy of wandering through lonely lands; the joy of hunting the mighty and terrible lords of the wilderness, the cunning, the wary, and the grim.
>
> "In these greatest of the world's great hunting-grounds there are mountain peaks whose snows are dazzling under the equatorial sun; swamps where the slime oozes and bubbles and festers in the steaming heat; lakes like seas; skies that burn above deserts where the iron desolation is shrouded from view by the wavering mockery of the mirage; vast grassy plains where palms and thorn-trees fringe the dwindling streams; mighty rivers rushing out of the heart of the continent through the sadness of endless marshes; forests of gorgeous beauty, where death broods in the dark and silent depths.
>
> "There are regions as healthy as the northland; and other regions, radiant with bright-hued flowers, birds and butterflies, odorous with sweet and heavy scents, but treacherous in their beauty, and sinister to human life. On the land and in the water there are dread brutes that feed on the flesh of man; and among the lower things, that crawl, and fly, and sting, and bite, he finds swarming foes far more evil and deadly than any beast or reptile; foes that kill his crops and his cattle, foes before which he himself perishes in his hundreds of thousands.
>
> "The dark-skinned races that live in the land vary widely. Some are warlike, cattle-owning nomads; some till the soil and live in thatched huts shaped like beehives; some are fisherfolk; some are ape-like naked savages, who dwell in the woods and prey on creatures not much wilder or lower than themselves.
>
> "The land teems with beasts of the chase, infinite in number and incredible in variety. It holds the fiercest beasts of ravin, and the fleetest and most timid of those beings that live in undying fear of talon and fang. It holds the largest and the smallest of hoofed animals. It holds the might-

iest creatures that tread the earth or swim in its rivers; it also holds distant kinsfolk of these same creatures, no bigger than woodchucks, which dwell in crannies of the rocks, and in the tree tops. There are antelope smaller than hares, and antelope larger than oxen. There are creatures which are the embodiments of grace; and others whose huge ungainliness is like that of a shape in a nightmare. The plains are alive with droves of strange and beautiful animals whose like is not known elsewhere; and with others even stranger that show both in form and temper something of the fantastic and the grotesque. It is a never-ending pleasure to gaze at the great herds of buck as they move to and fro in their myriads; as they stand for their noontide rest in the quivering heat haze; as the long files come down to drink at the watering-places; as they feed and fight and rest and make love.

"The hunter who wanders through these lands sees sights which ever afterward remain fixed in his mind. He sees the monstrous river-horse snorting and plunging beside the boat; the giraffe looking over the tree tops at the nearing horseman; the ostrich fleeing at the speed that none may rival; the snarling leopard and coiled python, with their lethal beauty; the zebras, barking in the moonlight, as the laden caravan passes on its night march through a thirsty land. In after years there shall come to him memories of the lion's charge; of the gray bulk of the elephant, close at hand in the sombre woodland; of the buffalo, his sullen eyes glowering from under his helmet of horn; of the rhinoceros, truculent and stupid, standing in the bright sunlight on the empty plain.

"These things can be told. But there are no words that can tell the hidden spirit of the wilderness, that can reveal its mystery, its melancholy, and its charm. There is delight in the hardy life of the open, in long rides rifle in hand, in the thrill of the fight with dangerous game. Apart from this, yet mingled with it, is the strong attraction of the silent places, of the large tropic moons, and the splendor of sunrise and sunset in the wide waste spaces of the earth, unworn of man, and changed only by the slow change of the ages through time everlasting."

Theodore Roosevelt

Khartoum, March 15, 1910

These are the carefully selected words of the President himself, not those of any ghost or speech writer. (See how we have progressed!)

These are words to stir the soul, and they stirred mine. The Africa of Theodore Roosevelt was an Africa unchanged, once one left the main road, since Díaz found his way to the Indian Ocean, since Van Riebeck landed at the Cape, or, for that matter, since Ptolemy's expedition circumnavigated it and Herodotus recounted its fables. *It was still there*, and I promised myself that I would go and see.

World War II may turn out to be the turning point of civilization as we know it. Before it, Africa was still a place one could do properly, as Streeter and Hemingway told us. Though not full grown when I read them, I still made plans. I learned to shoot, and practiced on everything handy, from Catalina goats on up. I grew and progressed, always dreaming of Africa. At last I bought a 375, and had ammunition packed for shipment. This was in 1939. Blooey!

Decades passed, with the physical and psychological changes that decades bring. Central Africa was terminated, as Britain abandoned the world and evil opportunists stepped into the political vacuum she left behind. To the south, the Republic of South Africa grew in wealth and sophistication, and in so doing thrust my enchanted wilderness largely into its past. It did seem that I was just too late—a half century on the wrong side of the watershed.

As it turned out—not quite.

There remained Rhodesia. Not "Zimbabwe," which is a fascinating ruined citadel, but *Rhodesia,* the work of Cecil John Rhodes, man of the West. Before Rhodes it lay almost empty, sparsely peopled by Mashona and Matabele, with pockets of Vendas, Manicas, Shangans, and others—all at perpetual and inconclusive war with each other. Rhodes brought in his own people and built a nation with a select following of civilized pioneers, and what he built did honor to the human race.

We look back upon those places and times in our history wherein life seemed good—at least in hindsight. They are never large nor lasting, but we envy the people who knew them. We can think upon the Vienna of The Congress, of Moorish Granada, of Edwardian Paris, of Tuckahoe Virginia or Arcadian California, and take pleasure. We can also look upon Rhodesia (1890-1979) with similar emotion. "Under the administration of Rhodes, there were the fewest laws, the widest freedom, the least crime, and the truest justice, that I have ever seen in any part of the world"—so wrote Frederick Russell Burnham, whose adventurous career gave him sound basis for his opinions. Rhodes died early in Rhodesia's history, but his principles were carried on by those who succeeded him. The late nation that bore his name was a very fine place indeed, in which the advantages of modern civilization were balanced marvelously against the ancient wonders of the wild.

Having missed the Great Africa of Theodore Roosevelt, it was my God-sent luck to catch Rhodesia—just before its demise. I must tell you about it.

Business called me to South Africa in 1974. Somewhat by chance, I was able to arrange a six-day visit to Salisbury. A minor bush war was underway along the Zambezi to the north, but it did nothing to mar the experience. It enhanced it, actually, in that it provided a truer understanding of social and political strife, advertised in the leftist press as racial but in fact a simple matter of Soviet imperialism.

I made it back again in '75, and this time for long enough to spend seven days with a rifle in the bush.

This was it. No "safari," in the classical sense, but still the realization of a long, long dream. Not a hundred meters from the ranch house, I looked up and saw—a giraffe! Everyone has seen a giraffe in a zoo, but the unreal aspect of this beast cannot hit you until you see him standing there in his own land, where he belongs and you do not.

A quarter mile farther we paused briefly and shot a warthog for the larder—just like that! The "wild boar" is a mighty prize in some places. On the Lundi River he is valued as provender—very tasty indeed, but "no big deal."

As we made camp on a bluff overlooking the river, I heard what I thought was a horse's snort at my elbow. It was indeed a sort of horse—a "river horse"—snorting two hundred meters away. A hippo—honest to God!

This was it. The kid who dreamed of Africa finally made it—as a grandfather. In seven days we saw thirteen different species of game. This may not sound overwhelming to a townsman, but to one who has hunted for a week in good deer country without spotting more than a jackrabbit, it was paradise enow. We shot very little and quite selectively. In a time when "bambiists" excoriate all hunters as monsters, it is well to remember the profound dictum of Ortega y Gasset: "One does not hunt in order to kill. One kills in order to have hunted."

We saw the lovely impala, by the hundreds. We met the comic zebra, the elfin bushbuck, the elegant kudu, the lordly eland. We found the ratel, the valorous "honey badger," and the bizarre red-and-silver bush pig. We glimpsed a princely leopard as he bounded across the trail in the headlights just before dawn. And, finally, we met "behemoth"—the deadly black buffalo.

Let's not have any confusion about the word "buffalo." It is of Greek origin (*Bouphalos*) and was originally applied to almost any sort of wild ungulate. Today it may refer to various wild oxen, including the Indian water buffalo (*Bubalus bubalis*) and the American bison (*Bison bison*), but to a hunter it denotes just one beast—*Synceros caffer*, the "Cape buffalo," though it has not been seen within a thousand miles of the Cape for generations. To each his own, but for me "buffalo" means *buffalo*—John Burger's "horned death."

The big black buff may be no more than vermin to some, but to me he is very grand. I relish everything about him, from his attitude to his steaks. And his horns, hung upon my terrace, recall to me great moments—the treasures of my memory.

The first meeting came very suddenly. We had hunted long and hard, and had passed up many opportunities to keep our primary goal in view. Then we met Terry, a game ranger on leave, and he told us that buff were no problem—just a matter of getting on with it.

On this occasion I was not properly armed. I was using a 350 carbine that started a 250 grain bullet at about 2,400 feet per second. These ballistics are not trivial, but I had available only soft-point, expanding bullets. Such bullets are excellent for lesser game, but for buffalo one needs "solids," which are heavily jacketed and will not deform on impact. None such were obtainable in this caliber at the time, and yet I felt that the piece might suffice. The combination had driven straight through the shoulder of a bull kudu, which is the size of an elk, without expansion. Would it then drive well into a buffalo? I put the question to Thys, a local cattleman.

"I couldn't say," he said. "I don't know your gun nor its cartridge. Once, however, I hit a buff squarely in the shoulder at short range with a 333 (also 250 at 2,500)—soft point. The bullet went in about three inches and flattened on the shoulder blade."

Hmm.

Well, the 350 was what I had, and buff have been known to drop to pistols, so I felt it might suffice. There is a small gravestone on the ranch commemorating a previous owner who had been killed by a buff that he had attacked with a 375 (300 at 2,500), but proper placement of the bullet is always more important than the power of the cartridge. It seemed worth a try. I asked Terry.

"Sure. Go ahead," he said. What he meant was that he, a professional, was going to be along with his 470, and that I was welcome to use a 22 if I chose. He didn't say it like that, but that's what he meant.

Hunting buffalo is not like hunting deer. The buff is not wary—why should he be?—but he is nervous. He likes to graze at night and bed down in thick cover during the day. In such cover he cannot be approached unaware. His nose is fine, but even if the wind is against him he will hear your movements before you can see him. He does not pick fights—normally—but he dislikes to be pushed. When he hears you he will move off—two or three hundred meters. If you approach again he will still probably move away, but his mood will change. On the third try he may not move—away.

But finding him is not the problem. Harvesting him, when found, is another matter. That we had not found him so far was due mainly to the fact that the local boys who had been "helping" us didn't *want* to find him. They came along for the meat, but you can get plenty of meat in Africa without tangling with *Nyati*. The lads can't really be blamed. They didn't know us, nor whether we could handle a rifle, and a wounded buff can't tell a rifleman from a tracker. No need to risk a pounding when there are so many antelope and pigs around.

It took us a while to figure this out, but after a few very obvious coughing fits and stick crackings we got the picture. But we still did not know how easy it is for a really good hunter to locate buff. For Terry it was a cinch.

We started late, and drove right to him. There, crossing the road, were his tracks, and they were fresh.

"Right in there," said Terry. "Carry on!"

Ray Chapman and I were the "sports," with Terry and Mike as support. We walked forward in a straight line and entered the thorn. It was perhaps eight feet high—visibility ten to forty meters, no shade, no wind.

The track was clear. Even I could follow it. We moved on, rifle at "high port," finger straight, safety on. We were quiet, but the buff heard us anyway. I could see nothing but the thorn and dry grass.

Then, oddly, I became aware of something. It was an odor. Not the barnyard reek of manure, but the strong, not unpleasant aroma of live, warm cattle close by. No sound. No sight. Just the immediate, intimate presence. We were right among them. I felt the hair rise on my neck.

You can't shoot what you can't see. But this is what you came to do. Live it! Forward—carefully. Carefully.

There! Left front. You've seen it in pictures, but this, now, is no picture. That's a *buffalo*—head up, nose on, staring right at you. He's moved as far as he is going to. Look at the massive head, at the black curving sweep of the great horns! The time is now!

Reflexively I dropped to kneeling, and lost him. Head-to-head we could just see each other, over the top of the intervening grass. If either ducked, the contact would be gone. It had to be offhand. No special problem on a target that size, at that distance.

The cross of the reticle stopped just under the black chin. Steady. No nerves. Steady. Now—gently—press—gently—CRASH.

The head dropped. Was he down?

CRASH, to my left rear.

The bull swung to his left and vanished.

"Come on!" shouted Terry and took off like a rabbit, bounding past me as he reloaded his double rifle on the run.

I started along as I worked the bolt, but not at a run. I am not used to shooting things that do not drop to the shot, and I just couldn't believe that the bull had not died in his tracks. The sight picture was good, the squeeze was good, the range was short. A 250 at 2,400, right in the gozzle. He's *got* to be down!

(As it happened, he wasn't even hurt much. He had not been standing straight on, but at an angle that I could not see. The bullet entered where I intended but slipped to one side of the throat channel, entered the heavy neck muscle, mushroomed to about 55 caliber, drove in some eighteen inches, and stopped. A stiff neck—nothing more.)

Terry's back-up shot, delivered from behind me, had raked him diagonally as he wheeled. The 500-grain 470 bullet had entered over the right hip and stopped forward of the left shoulder, but the bull paid it no attention.

Terry and Ray had both passed me and I tried to catch up, but before I could do so the end came. The mortally wounded buff turned to charge and, as it did so, Terry, from a dead run, slammed to a stop and placed his bullet almost exactly between the eyes as the head was turned to gore. I am looking at the skull as I write. The huge bullet hole completes a cyclopian mask. That was the finest offhand shot I have ever seen.

So, at last, I met *Nyati*. The occasion was, except for Terry's marvelous shot, unremarkable, but I was personally impressed. To hunt buffalo became Objective A; and it still is.

The fascination of the hunt is multifarious. Tastes differ marvelously. While some men take joy in any sort of hunting, others specialize. To one there is nothing to match the pursuit of the magnificent wild sheep, high and holy, the spirit of the roof of the world. To another the fabled *Auerhahn*, ghost of the ancient depths of European forests, is the unequaled quarry. To a third the ability to walk up undetected on a fully mature whitetail buck—season after season—is the only measure of a real hunter. For me there is the buffalo.

Synceros caffer—the joined-horned infidel—just happens to epitomize all my personal preferences. He is plentiful, succulent, cunning, irascible, vengeful, unbelievably strong, and nearly invulnerable to inept marksmanship. He is there, he is choice, he is ready, and he will do his impressive best to kill you if you bother him. To follow him into a thicket, as you often must, is to live richly. I am very glad that I hunted long and widely, over many decades, before I met *Nyati*. It would have been a misfortune to have started with him and have had to work down.

This obsession of mine is by no means universal, or even common. An older generation of African hunters held the buffalo to be little more than an edible varmint—a dangerous nuisance that ate up the range, got in the way, and carried cattle diseases. Many moderns have dropped their buff without drama and gone on to scarcer or more elegant game. That's fine. To each his own. I just have this private feeling about *Synceros*, and I don't feel any great need to share it. I have met him. I treasure the experience. And I will repeat it as long as I can.

It is often said that the buffalo is the most dangerous of those animals classified as "dangerous game." This may or may not be true in an absolute sense, though it probably is statistically. Certainly the lion is faster, the elephant is stronger, the leopard more cunning, and the rhino readier to attack. The tiger has his special niche, and the great bears have "chewed up and spit out" a lot of good men. But unlike the elephant and rhino, the buff will not be turned, once he has a target on the screen. Unlike the lion and leopard, bullets hardly faze him. Unlike the bears, he will not leave his victim alive. He doesn't start trouble, but he is happy to oblige if offended, and his wrath is terrible.

Those who do not understand these things generally sneer at the hunter's joy in meeting him. "What danger?" they ask. "You have a powerful rifle. All you do is shoot, and he falls down. What chance has he? What sort of contest is that?"

Obviously we don't change a mind already made up, but the subject is not as easily dismissed as all that.

Peril—not variety—is the spice of life. As with salt, or any other condiment you fancy, too much is bad, but not enough is not good either. A surfeit of peril is demoralizing, but a life with none at all is flat indeed. No one can enjoy life fully without looking now and then squarely into the face of death. After a near miss the air is fresher, the sun brighter, food richer, wine more fragrant, a bath more refreshing, a bed softer, and love sweeter—*because we are vividly aware of what we almost lost.* There is nothing obscure or complicated about this, and no one who has lived strenuously needs it explained to him. We may feel sorry, however, for the unenlightened.

The important thing about dangerous sports is that we choose them. To carry out dangerous work because we must is one thing, but freely to seek a challenge which may well result in death is quite another. Danger is truly the spice of life. Some like it spicier than others. A certain kind of man, evidently, feels ashamed of fears that do not trouble another. He may indeed seek deliberately to confront his fears and so to overcome them. Such a man is fighting his own private battle, but he is not typical of all those who play with danger. Many simply prefer a bit more pepper in the stew.

So when a hunter takes after the great black buffalo of Africa he is not indulging a "death wish" or any such psychiatric cant—he is just enjoying life fully. He does not claim that he will *probably* meet with disaster—*probably* he won't—but he just *might*. As with mountaineering, motor racing, hang gliding, scuba diving, or rodeo riding—he *probably* won't but he *might*.

The special thing about *Synceros* is that you can't be certain of your blow. Unless you brain him, no hit—anywhere, with anything—will always bring him down. If he is hit and drops, O.K. That is the humane objective. But if the buff is hit and charges, then the hunter sees death climbing right up his nose, and if the charge is stopped he has looked him in the eye and faced him down. This is a very simple and very grand feeling.

If a buffalo is hit and does not drop, he usually does not "run up the gun." More often he bolts laterally into cover and seeks his enemy. When he attacks he picks out one man, locks on him, and stays with him until one or the other is dead. This is why a hunter is sometimes knocked aside with only minimal injuries. *Nyati* had not chosen him. There have been cases where a buff tossed a man so far in thick cover that he couldn't find him again, and so the man lived. But if a buff chooses you, gets to you, and knocks you down—that's it.

To quote Jack Lott, "With buffalo it's not enough just to kill him. You have to make him understand that he has undergone a change of status, and that is sometimes not easy." Jack had a rare donnybrook with a bull some years back and is lucky to have survived. He speaks with feeling.

It is perhaps best to have only a moderate number of experiences with *Synceros*. Anything can lose its glamor if done to excess, and I am sure that the pros who cull buffalo for wages have lost the exhilaration that I know now. This is doubly fortunate for me, because it is said that a man's hundredth buff is the one that will probably kill him, and if I can arrange to confront twenty more in my life I will be very lucky.

Around African campfires the talk ever turns to "dangerous game"—those beasts of the chase that can, and do—occasionally—kill their human assailants. Africa has the largest variety of such creatures to be found anywhere, ranging in size from the pachyderms to a fine selection of venomous snakes, which, while not game animals, can be distinctly lethal.

It is great fun to wax comparative on this topic—which beast is *most* dangerous?— the more so because no conclusion may be reached. The ingenuous usually leap to statistics, and it is always possible to find some list, somewhere, that will verify a preformed opinion, but peril is essentially a state of mind, and does not lend itself to statistical analysis. We are all equally in peril since we will all eventually die. It's not a matter of whether, but how? Thus "the most dangerous game," to any individual, is simply that which scares him the most. Naturally, any man who has ever been caught by anything will feel that *that* beast was the prize winner.

It is nonetheless possible to discern a pattern of probabilities. Certain kinds of people are indeed more likely to "meet with an accident" as the victims of certain kinds of animals. (In most cases, of course, it is no accident on the part of the animal.)

The hippopotamus, for example, is not thought of as a hazard, and ordinarily he is not—to a hunter. But he is a terror to native women who go to the stream for water in the dawn. The hippo spends his days in the river and comes out to graze at night, traveling as much as a mile from his base. As the sky lightens he heads back, increasingly nervous as the sun approaches. If he tarries overlong with his feeding he may be in something of a panic, and woe to anything standing in his path to the water! Thus, according to one set of statistics, the hippo is clearly the most dangerous animal in Africa.

But hippos do not prey upon native children—it's leopards that do that. The "natural" food of the leopard is the baboon, living in packs and quite tough when collectively aroused. (Baboons share most of the worst characteristics of humanity.) The leopard must approach with great care, studying the behavior of his target group, striking and vanishing in a flash, and selecting a small target that will not offer much resistance. The parallel is obvious.

The rhinoceros has his own specialty—the photographer. Photographers tend to be rather innocent and do not expect a "scene," unlike hunters, who do. When a photographer spots a rhino, standing out on the plain engaged in dim Pleistocenic cogitation, his first thought is naturally for the great picture he can get. He intends the beast no harm and assumes that this feeling must therefore be mutual. Totally preoccupied with available light, background, framing, filters, and such, he advances blithely to his task, eye glued to view-finder. Presently he discovers that his view-finder is rapidly filling up with his subject—horn first. At this point, not being a hunter, his response is often to turn and run. This is the wrong response. A rhino is not bright, nor very agile, and his eyesight is poor. He can, however, run faster than any photographer, and he is unlikely to lose sight of a target moving straight away—legs churning, arms flailing, and cameras dangling.

The obvious quarry of the crocodile is the Peace Corps. These young people are fond of swimming, and forbidden by contract to be armed. The locals usually know better than to swim in unscreened water without a rifleman on guard. *Que será, será.*

The elephant seems to be a prime danger to tourists—especially youth groups. Such gay parties seem to think that elephants are "cute." And so they are, in many ways, but to be cute is not necessarily to be kind. One should not play with elephants. At such time as an elephant feels that either his privacy or his dignity is affronted he may very well take a notion to slap the affronter with his trunk. An elephant slap is no light matter. And, of course, there are cows with calves. Very touchy. The proper course is to stand well back from elephants, but these youth groups rarely heed. I witnessed a disaster of this sort in the making in one of the parks some time ago. Fortunately nothing serious actually happened, but it drove the game ranger who was with me pretty well round the bend.

The lion, certainly, can be a terrible thing. Four-hundred pounds of high-velocity cat, beautifully equipped for killing, he occupies a traditional niche as the ancient and honored foe of man. A lion's charge is one of the wonders of the world, and to be caught by him must certainly be a shocking experience. People are sometimes caught but not killed—no one but the lion can say why—and the ultimate stroke in one-upmanship is the casual exhibition of the resulting scars, with the comment, "But you will never *really* understand Africa until you have been mauled by a lion." What can you say to that?

Lions are unique among Africa's "big four" in that they need not be pestered in order to be deadly. They will frequently hunt, kill and eat people entirely on their own initiative. This happenstance is not as rare as the bambiists would prefer to believe. A lion—any lion—is definitely anthropophagous, and it is well to keep this in mind when prowling the bundu. That a human being may be deliberately sought out and claimed as food is a gruesome and upsetting thought, and it sets the lion apart. But he doesn't specialize, he eats black and white, young and old, soldier and civilian, hunter and hunter-hater—all with equal relish. In agreement with Will Rogers, the lion attests "I never met a man I didn't like."

Unique in still another sense, the lion hits when you are *not ready.* With elephant and rhino you meet your antagonist gun-in-hand. The man-eating lion arrives when you are cooking, or reading, or dozing—preferably when you are asleep. Your rifle may be a marvel, but it is no help then.

Yes, lions may not specialize, but they *are* special.

And what of *Nyati,* our great and good friend the buffalo? A majority of the people I have read and talked to give him the place of honor, but I think this is due to the consensus that more *hunters* are totalled by buffalo than by other animals. This in turn may be because more buffalo are there to hunt. They have always been plentiful everywhere, until the advent of black power in Africa, and they still are in some places. And they are very good to eat. This leads to a lot of cases involving incompetence and inadequate armament. Skilled men, properly armed and operating in pairs, are (statistically) pretty safe from buffalo; but these conditions do not always obtain. Vilhjalmar Steffanson once told a class I attended that "Adventure is always the result of incompetence." I found this dictum depressing, as stated, but I came to understand that what he meant was that if you always do everything right you'll never have any trouble. This is true, but people—even excellent people—do not always do everything right. We do our best, or we should, but that is sometimes not enough.

Thus if a man never makes a mistake he will never have trouble with a buffalo, nor with anything else. Let him who has never made a mistake feel smug. It does seem, nonetheless, that the special target of the buffalo is the hunter.

The venomous snakes of Africa do not pick on particular target groups. Like all snakes, they would prefer to be left alone. But bare legs, black or white, certainly make it easy for them, and bare legs are *in* in Africa. I think the great Selous started this fad among white men, but it was routine with the Bantu since before they started south from the Sudan. In my opinion, bare legs in the bush are an open invitation to septicemia—anywhere in the world. (As a youth I dutifully read scores of British colonials on what-to-do-about-leeches. Never occurred to them to keep their pants on.)

Among the snakes pride of place goes to *Dendraspis,* the mamba. If he is not the deadliest snake in the world he is certainly the most fearsome. He is both big and very toxic, but what seems to make his reputation is his speed of movement, combined with a sort of nervous aggressiveness. No, he can't "run as fast as a horse," but he is astonishingly fast for a snake. No, he does not "charge unprovoked," but he will often move quickly forward into a better striking position. He does indeed kill people, often very experienced people. He killed a noted professional hunter a year prior to my first visit.

I've been an amateur ophiologist since youth, and I told Paul that I would dearly love to encounter a mamba in the wild. "Would you now?" he replied. "Well, I wouldn't." And Paul has wrestled with dangerous game for all his adult life.

There are other snakes—many cobras (including the spitting variety), the imposing Gaboon Viper, the Rhinoceros Viper, the ubiquitous puff adder (which occupies exactly the same ecological niche as the American rattlesnakes) and the common and highly toxic Boomslang.

Growing up in a land full of rattlesnakes, I am accustomed to sluggish vipers, not slithery elapids. Vipers hold still and you can easily pop them in the head, but cobras are another matter. They dodge. Invited to shoot a cobra on the pistol range at Johannesburg, I took four shots to connect! It was a ringhals (pronounced "Ring—clear the throat—als"), the spitting sort, so I thought it well to stand a bit back. Range fifteen feet, target the size of a pigeon egg. Every time I squeezed he ducked. This went on and on. It was hilarious to assorted spectators but it made me feel silly. The cobra eventually lost, but my reputation was severely tarnished. Also I expended three rounds of my host's 45 ammunition uselessly, a pretty serious matter in embargoed Africa.

There are other things as well—wild dogs, hyenas, warthogs, and even gorillas are said to have killed people; and among the antelope sable, roan and bushbucks should be approached with care. Yes, it's still a rifleman's wilderness—the last in this world.

With buffalo as my main quest, I was able to meet with several, and each occasion was memorable. Some are recounted elsewhere in this collection. But it was not until the last that I really soaked up the essence of the buffalo hunt. This was not a successful episode, but it does stay with me.

On this occasion Paul had in mind to take a "spare" buffalo to use as lion bait, and if there was a chance of improving upon the one I had taken I wished to get into it. He had spotted a bunch earlier in the day and there was little trouble in making a reasonable approach. As usual they were located in a thick patch of Jessie thorn. It is something like a hedge, and hunting in it is next to impossible. Each time we made contact we were too close to see what we had. We could smell the animals and we knew that they knew that we were there, but we couldn't quite make each other out. In the first instance, the heads we saw were too small to justify. They got our wind and ran. We made another approach. This time Paul made out a very large one but I could not, since the intervening brush was too thick, and they made off again.

There is nothing in hunting to approach the follow-up of Cape buffalo in dense cover. It's one of the most exhilarating experiences known. It should not be compared exactly to finding a needle in a haystack—since the matter of locating the animals is not that difficult. It is more like trying to find a land mine in a supermarket. A buffalo is a big animal and if you are in the right area you will see him. The question is— what then?

As the sun rose it became hotter. We moved through the thorn, cutting our- selves, losing our hats, keeping low, and again we made contact with the herd. This time they spooked laterally and I almost got a shot. The front sight was on the shoulder of a very large bull as he moved to my right when the muzzle swung onto Paul standing ahead of me and I could not shoot. We had been at this for two hours and more and, while the joy was still there, exhaustion had begun to take its toll. I whispered to Paul, "It's too bloody thick." His answer, "*I can shoot one.*" My response, "O.K. If I get a chance I'll take it but if you see them first, go ahead." We proceeded on that basis.

More sneaking through the thorn. The tracks are fresh. The droppings are fresh. We can smell the animals. They are there. They are big. And we can find them. Back and forth we move. Hour after hour. The patch of ground is perhaps 300 acres in extent and the buff move ahead of us when they sense us. Tradition has it that buff will only move twice. The third time they will stand and attack. But not today. Our faces and hands are scratched and the legs of Paul and Samson, which are bare, are bloody to the socks. We keep trying. The buff keep moving. Finally, ahead of us, a black mountain. Paul stands up to shoot. I move to support him. He presses. The weapon bobs. The safety is on. He slips the safety off. I can't make out which is which on the animal— that is to say which end is facing right or left. I am not sure. Paul fires. The buffalo bounces—we can see hoofs in the air. He is down, he is up. *It was the wrong end!*

There is blood, and we follow. And we follow. The thorn is dense The attack may come from any direction. This is a very intense experience. Paul and Samson watch for tracks and blood. I try to maintain a 360-degree alert. This is the classic followup of the wounded buffalo. The tension is extreme.

Over the edge of a bank and down into deep grass. Now the range is measured in feet rather than yards. From any direction it may come. We lose the blood, but we follow.

I am not exactly frightened, but I am immensely preoccupied. I know the destruc- tive power of the rifle in my hands and I know that Paul is an experienced marksman. It's not so much the feeling that one may be killed in the next instant, but whether or not one does the right job. I try to make sure of my rifle's condition. I have long since taken off the sling strap. I carry the weapon at high port, finger straight, thumb on the safety. I try to watch every way at once. My concern is where on that huge black body to place the bullet. Where? Exactly what spot? He may come from any di- rection and I can stop him, but I have to do it right. Concentration is fierce. The silence is deafening. I can almost hear the sweat running down my nose.

Nothing.

We lost him. We're all played out. I am very tired and even Paul and Samson are showing signs of fatigue. We secure. The bull must be found, but after lunch, with more help. We head back to camp. Out.

After lunch we were well and truly bushed. Our clothes were torn and Paul's legs were a bloody mess. Noting this, Ray volunteered to go back and look for the wounded bull and I didn't feel up to arguing with him.

As it turned out, they found the buffalo (the herd) not ten minutes after they had left the truck. Paul shot one, but it turned out to be the wrong buffalo. It would serve well enough for lion bait, but it would not do anything about the hazard posed by a wounded buffalo wandering through the brush looking for somebody to stomp. However there was nothing to be done and the chase was abandoned since Paul had to arrange to get the new buff into position where it would attract a lion for Raul.

Failure, but still an event to remember.

This may be one of the last hunts before the lights go out all over Africa. There is no hunting anymore in the good game country to the North, for various reasons. When black racist dictatorships take over they usually arm the peasantry and eliminate the game. If racist tyranny is indeed imposed upon southern Africa, as both East and West seem to wish, there will be no more hunting in this greatest of the world's great hunting grounds. Its termination will be just one among the numerous tragedies which are in store for Africa if the communists win. The world knows—or it should—what happens when the enemy takes over. How long South Africa can hold out now that Rhodesia is gone is moot, but it will not be indefinitely. The greatest tragedy is that this destruction of all western values is coming about, not through the *inability* of the West to defend itself, physically or technically, but because of its loss of morale. We just don't *want* to win. God knows there are millions of us who do, but our millions are not enough to control events.

In light of all this the elimination of hunting from the world is a fairly minor consideration. But hunting as a recreation is one of those traditions that we truly prize—we who are left of the free people of the world. Our other traditions, such as the right of privacy, the right to individual enterprise, the rights to the fruits of our own labor, the right to be let alone by our governments, the right to criticize our governments, and the right to move freely throughout the world, all these are in no better shape than our right to go hunting. This Kariba hunt I have just spoken of may well be the last hunt. Despite its inconveniences, it was a magnificent experience and we must praise to the skies our hosts for their courtesy, thoughtfulness and generosity in making it possible at a time when they were fighting with their backs to the wall against injustice and expropriation. We thank them and salute them, and we will do the best we can to spread the word.

154

FireWorks

22

Baby

IF ONE TAKES A COMPLETELY UTILITARIAN VIEW of rifles he concerns himself only with what he really needs, or what his customers or clients need. It is abundantly clear, however, that this pragmatic approach to firearms is not universal, nor even common. Perhaps, to a dedicated shooter, the needs of the soul surpass those of the mind, for look at all the really frivolous guns we buy, sell, handle, admire, and lust after! Firearms are tools, but they are also toys. For a lot of people, life would be grey indeed without toys. Nobody *needs* a full stereo set. Nobody *needs* handcarved chessmen, nor an expensive wristwatch, nor a water bed, nor high-fashion clothes, nor even opera tickets. Certainly nobody really *needs* a Ferrari. But we *want* these things. It may be that we enjoy wanting them fully as much as having them. To transcend desire may be Nirvana, but Nirvana may be Dullsville.

So, after my first trip to Africa, I came to lust after a heavy rifle. Not just *any* heavy rifle, but a heavy rifle of my own design. (So I didn't need a heavy rifle. Understood. But I wanted one very badly.) I had shot a few. I saw them in action on dangerous game. I went back and read all the "authorities" again, and spent many cheerful hours in bull sessions. Gradually it became apparent that, while many of the ready-made versions were quite satisfactory, the path to true joy lay in conceiving, assembling, testing, and finally hunting with an eclectic synthesis of my own creation. This would take months, even years, to bring off, and the effort would be a prolonged delight. In a small and limited way it would be an act of creation, and the creation of something splendid, to be proven in splendid action. The idea took hold (obviously) and I set about the realization of "Baby," an idealized heavy rifle.

The mission of the heavy rifle is the killing of very large, dangerous animals under difficult conditions. If the conditions are not difficult the same job can be done as well with a medium rifle, or so it is said. My personal experience with dangerous game is not extensive, but even so I have seen two instances where a medium was well handled but did not suffice. There are authenticated cases where a heavy did not suffice either, but let it pass. The object of *this* exercise was a heavy.

With the creeping demise of big game hunting, heavies are even less common now than they were in the early part of the century, and they were not in any sense a mass product then. Still, or perhaps therefore, the heavies are very interesting. Their sheer power is awesome, many are magnificent works of art, most are astonishingly accurate, and they are really great fun to shoot—for some people.

Let us then define a "heavy" rifle. We do not refer to its own weight, but rather to the weight of the blow it delivers, and this is a function of the cartridge it fires. This cartridge should be of more than 10mm caliber (.40"), its missile should weigh about or above one English ounce (437 grains) and should exit the muzzle at somewhat more than 2,000 feet per second. Its kinetic energy is thus 5,000 ft/lbs or more, but let us not dwell overlong on k.e., which is demonstrably unsatisfactory as an index of impact effect.

The most powerful shoulder rifles I know of are the 510 Wells (700 at 2,500), the 475 A&M (600 at 2,500), the 460 Weatherby (500 at 2,700) and the 600 Nitro (900 at 1,950). These velocities are as claimed by the designers, and vary considerably with loadings and barrel length. At this upper end of the power scale we are encountering around 250 pounds of recoil, and while I once fired a 510 Wells twelve times, I did not wish to try for twenty.

Like most Americans, I was raised to be recoil shy. It was not until middle life that I learned that recoil discomfort is far more a matter of stock design than of sheer punch. Not that the big guns don't kick. They do. But only a few kick so hard as to disturb a seasoned marksman in good physical condition.

But it is not necessary to go too far. The standard 470 Nitro and 458 Winchester start 500-grain bullets at around 2,050, and, in well stocked rifles, they are surprisingly pleasant to shoot. There is a good, solid rearward surge, but the muzzle rises only four or five inches at peak when the piece is fired from the offhand position. I once saw Tony Weeks shoot a cloverleaf (three shots touching) at 100 meters, off a bench, with an open-sighted 458, and Tony is not a big man.

The big guns come in double-barrelled and bolt-action configurations, and while a lot of people feel very strongly that one or the other type is incomparably superior, either will do—in skilled hands.

The double is shorter and handier. Its rate of fire is higher—in the short and in the extended run, though not for five or six shots. Also, with a double you know exactly how many rounds you have left, whereas with a magazine rifle you can lose count; and a double cannot "jam." A double can be dismayingly expensive, but, as with yachts, if you have to ask the price you really can't afford one anyway.

On the other hand, the technique of the double is a bit tricky, and must be learned well before putting one's self in harm's way. Not only do the two triggers call for different directional pressure, but reloading at a dead run without looking at the breech takes practice. And that problem *does* arise. It occurred on our first contact with buff in thick brush.

Having cut my teeth on a bolt gun, and being too old a dog for new tricks, I chose the bolt—but that is not to say that a good double might not be a better weapon in the hands of a man who knows all about it.

When the time finally came to select a heavy, my first thought was the 505 Gibbs. Fifty caliber, 535 grains, recoil about half-way between the 458 and the 460 Weatherby—in guns of equal weight. Five shots without a reload. And this piece has a fine reputation in Africa. A fifty caliber bullet has about 1/3 more impact area than a 45. Solid (FMJ) bullets are all we expect to use on buff, and the size of the wound channel is a function of the square of the caliber—assuming full penetration.

But the old Gibbs is obsolete. Any individual example I might find would be an antique, made to another man's specifications and very difficult to feed. Custom ammunition is not the problem with a heavy rifle that it may be with a medium, but proper bullets for a charge-stopping cartridge are not made in all sizes.

After hearing of several failures with the fifties, in which a solid broke up on heavy bone, and during the same period hearing nothing but good about the excellent 45 caliber solids of Winchester and Hornady, I somewhat reluctantly opted for a 45. The rationale was that if one has "enough" why does one need "more." (This despite Mae West's famed dictum to the effect that, "Too much of a good thing is . . . . marvelous!")

The first thing was to choose a cartridge. The "458 Winchester Magnum" is world standard and usually performs very well, but one hears complaints. It is an improvisation, made by blowing out the H&H case to .458". This makes it straight sided, nose-heavy, and a bit skimpy in powder capacity. One hears of its cramping when fed at maximum speed, due to the geometric problem of aligning a long, straight cartridge with a long, straight chamber by double deflection. All the weight forward aggravates this. Then there is the belt at the case head, made to control headspace but not necessary with a bottle-necked cartridge, and constituting another protrusion to interlock if two rounds are improperly positioned in the magazine. Reliable feeding is a life-or-death matter in a heavy, unlike a deer gun, and *almost* right is not enough. By choice the cartridge for a magazine-fed heavy should be balanced further aft than the 458 and should be conical rather than cylindrical, with a distinct shoulder and no belt. A somewhat larger powder bottle will do no harm. There is such a cartridge. It is the "460 G&A" invented some years ago by Tom Siatos by necking the 404 Jeffery up to 45. It is a proven round, used with excellent success by African game rangers. It is ballistically more versatile than the 458, offering higher velocities with the same bullet in long barrels, and a still better edge in short barrels. New, unfired brass is available from RWS, occasionally from Norma, and on order from Brass Extrusion Laboratories.

The special 460 lies almost exactly halfway between the 458 and the Weatherby. If we were to use the old U.S. system of cartridge designation (and used #4064 powder) we would call the 458 a "46/75," the special a "46/90," and the Weatherby a "46/105," as those are normal charges for the standard 500-grain bullet. Velocities, in 24" barrels, run about 2,100, 2,400, and 2,700. If one favors a short barrel on a "charge stopper," as I do, the 458 begins to look a little tired, whereas, on the other hand, shoving that great bullet out to 2,700 would seem to add nothing that the target could discern while increasing both recoil and cartridge bulk. If we stay above about 2,200 f/s initially we have all the impact effect and penetration we can use. Velocities higher than that serve mainly to flatten trajectory, and a heavy is primarily a short-range weapon. Even if we find it necessary to take an unusually long shot, available trajectory differentials are not very significant on a target the size of a buffalo. If the 500 at 2,200 is zeroed for 150 yards, for example, it will print about 1¾" high at 100 (less at 50) and only 5½" low at 200. If we start that same bullet at 2,700 those figures read 1¼" and 4". Who cares?

The upshot is that the 46/90 seems a very nice combination of desiderata. To quote Jack Lott:

> "The .460 G&A is a better balanced round than either the .460 Weatherby or .458, which has mediocre and inconsistent penetration due to short case and compressed (heavily) powder load. Sometimes it penetrates deeply and then another shot at a similar animal at the same angle results in shallow penetration. I have collected overwhelming evidence to show that the .458 is a defective design and has caused many, many incidents in which game was wounded due to failure of the round. Naturally the factories refuse to accept responsibility for the problem and will say something like, 'You didn't take good care of your ammo, left it on the dashboard in hot sun, etc.' "

I find that many other African users of 458's are increasingly unhappy with factory loads. They relate disturbing case histories, and they now roll their own. If you are going to do that you may as well use a wildcat as long as you can obtain bullets, and new cases once in a while.

With any "wildcat," the question of ammunition supply arises. Is it not better to choose a standard round, which can be bought over the counter? For a utility gun, a survival gun, any sort of general purpose gun, the answer is yes, always. But a heavy is not any of these things. It is highly specialized, and it is not shot so much that feeding it becomes a serious problem. If you build 200 rounds to go with your heavy they are likely to last a long time. Allowing 50 for testing, 150 shots at elephant, buffalo, and lion are quite a lot. A man could hunt a long time without denting that supply very much.

So the 460 G&A, a "460 Special," was settled upon as Baby's caliber.

Baby's action was much harder to select. It is said that before you begin to hunt

Bongo you must first find an 'Ndorobo tracker. Likewise before you start to build your pet heavy rifle you must locate a proper action. Wells, of Prescott, can build you one from scratch, if you can afford that sort of money and can wait that long, but I had neither the time nor the money.

The first 460 G&A was built on the old Remington 30 action, mainly for reasons of reliability. A broad, claw extractor and a positive ejector are deemed best for positive functioning, and are not to be found on many modern bolt actions. Additionally, most such are far too slim to accept five, fat Jeffery cartridges.

You don't find five-shot magazines in current production 458's. The Mannlicher and Remington hold four, the rest only three. And the larger diameter of the Jeffery case will cut that to two in most cases.

I am aware of the creed of the one-shot kill. I agree that it is every true sportsman's goal. I hope that I never get anything else when I fire—but I also know that things do not always turn out as planned. A perfectly hit buffalo drops to the shot about half the time. The other occasions must be prepared for. Buffalo hunting in thick brush is more like combat than the chase, and can easily degenerate into a vulgar brawl. I want six rounds in the piece, whether or not one shot ought to be enough.

The action we decided upon, after study and discussion, was (of all things!) the Czech Brno ZKK 602. This provided nearly all the essentials, plus a few extras, without any of those "modern conveniences" which are advertised as advantages while actually being no more than manufacturing shortcuts. Every knowledgeable gunmaker I consulted agreed that the ZKK #600 series Brno (600 regular, 601 short, and 602 magnum) is the last and best of the Mauser-type bolt actions. Frank de Haas, in *Bolt Action Rifles*, says,

> "The ZKK action cannot be described as merely 'an improved M98 Mauser' action, for it is much more than that. It does have some M98 features, but it has so many more that are not as to make it distinct."

It is very strong, very smooth, very reliable. Everything is designed for solidity and simplicity, without extra cuts or moving parts. It may be single-loaded above the magazine (a significant point of capacity), and it has no frills apart from its excellent built-in aperture sight which, in Baby's case, was more a necessity than a frill.

Brno firearms and parts are not normally imported into the U.S., but problems are made to be solved. These actions can be had—legally—by purchasers who won't take no for an answer, though it does take a bit of doing.

But the magazine of the ZKK 602 will still not accommodate five big cases. My heart was set on a six-shooter, however, and if you can find the right man custom machine work can do wonders.

I found the right man. Georg Hoenig, of Boise, is not only a distinguished classical gunsmith but he has an interest in the 460 cartridge, having worked on the first rifles made for it. He was therefore asked to do the assembly work on the project and he built an extension magazine that is flawless, in both design and execution.

Having selected the cartridge and the action, a barrel was next on the list. It was ordered from Douglas, of such dimensions that it would add up to an 11½ pound rifle and still be only 21" long. It came out thick. This thickness causes astonishment, and some esthetic pain to some people. (Handsome is as handsome does, however, and the result does very handsomely indeed.)

The figure of 11½ pounds was arbitrary, but based upon my own field experience plus a little pencil work. What was wanted was a piece that was appreciably more potent than a 458 but which would kick somewhat less. We got it.

Most 458's have 24" barrels; the Mannlicher goes 26.5" and the Remingtons and early Winchesters had 26's. Most current 458's weigh in at about 9 pounds (except the Colt Sauer which goes 10½). This does not seem the best arrangement to me. I prefer a short, burly bruiser to a long, light one. Any heavy is essentially a brush gun, and may even occasionally be used at arm's length. The big guns do kick, if not as much as you may have heard, so a bit of extra weight serves to soak up the jolt. With the big case the 21" 460 will beat a 24" 458 by almost 200 f/s, and its apparent recoil in an 11½ pound piece is slightly less than that of a nine-pound 458. Specifically, if we take Speer #9 as our guide, a factory 458 starts a 500-grain solid from a 24" barrel at 2,080 f/s. The 460 clocks 2,260 in 21" with the same bullet. If we use momentum as our index of recoil, the former shows 148.5 pounds, and the latter 161.4. If we divide the momentum of the projectile by the weight of the respective pieces, we get an index of 16.5 for a nine-pound 458, and 14.0 for the eleven-and-a-half pound 460—or a reduction of some 15%. This can be adjusted considerably by stock design, and with a custom stock made for me personally the apparent edge should be, if anything, increased.

Baby's sights, like everything else about her, were the result of much cogitation, some of it radical. Traditionally the sights on a heavy rifle are of the "express" variety— a medium or coarse gold bead matched to a shallow open V. Fast, but imprecise. This is fine for 80% of the work you may put a heavy to, but you might do well to think about that exceptional long shot. It can come up, as I will relate later. (I confess that open sights—on a rifle—defeat me. Some people use them very well, I have heard, but for me they provide no accurate index of elevation.)

With the general adoption of the telescope sight in the decades following W.W. II, people have generally abandoned the aperture sight on sporting arms, and a whole generation has forgotten how to use it. The non-traditional heavy now sports a glass, which is all very well, but on Baby we chose that form of aperture called the "ghost ring."

The telescope is fine, of course. Sharp, single-plane index, superior dim-light performance, excellent speed when understood, and accommodation to failing eyesight. It is also quite strong, in good examples. Still, a scope does encumber a rifle. Its lenses must be kept clean—possibly a problem in a thicket—and while unquestionably an advantage in a deliberate shot, it can sometimes be blanked in a whirl-and-fire situation at ten feet. And now, after having used both kinds of sights on dangerous game, I do wonder if the advantages of a scope are not more theoretical than practical in these particular circumstances. Game animals that can kill you are big targets—you don't need to magnify them.

As it happens, good hunting apertures are very rare today, but the ZKK 602 comes with one built right into its receiver bridge. It is neat, adjustable, and very strong. The orifice as furnished is too small for fast work, but it can be opened to proper diameter in seconds. "Peep" sights, with pinhole orifices and much metal surrounding them, are popular with target shooters but a drag in the field. What is wanted on a hunting rifle, especially on a charge-stopper, is this ghost ring—a large aperture with very little metal in its circumference. Such a sight is very quick and, if a square front post is used, very accurate. Regardless of what the target shot may tell you, it is *not* imprecise. A man who shoots better with a pinhole than with a ghost ring just does not know how to use a ghost ring. (Here on the ranch we shoot 22 offhand on our three-distance course almost every day. There are many guests, with many degrees of skill. Observation has made me quite sure about the scoring potential of the ghost ring, and there is no argument about its speed.)

So a rather small (1/16") square post with a gold face was ordered out front, and the opened (¼") rear aperture was retained. No scope mounting problems. No top-hamper. Efficiency with simplicity!

Baby was to be stocked in straightforward fashion, from a sound and husky blank of English walnut. Hoenig was asked to build it to my specs, keeping it straight, thick, and solidly bedded against double recoil lugs. I asked for plain but careful checkering, recessed sling swivels (a Pachmayr exclusive), a plain rubber butt cushion, and a classic oil finish. Slings of any kind are scorned in Africa, and indeed a shooting sling does seem a touch superfluous on a heavy, but I pack my own rifle, especially in Africa and especially now, and a carrying strap is handy on the hike back to base. You don't fancy gashing your left hand on a swivel stud when 90 grains of 4064 is lit behind 500 grains of bullet, so these flush attachments are both pretty *and* useful.

The object of the exercise was the creation of a specialty rifle of Doric simplicity and total efficiency, whose beauty, exemplifying the dictum that form follows function, would shine forth even to those who neither know nor care about fine guns. I did not spare expense, but neither did I do anything extravagant (apart from initiating the whole project). The best of everything was stipulated, without decoration or ornament of any kind.

This was the concept. I pushed the necessary buttons and sat back to wait. George Hoenig, master armorer, took over.

After a good many months of epicurean anticipation, punctuated by testy phone calls, the job was finished. Doctor Hoenig packed it up and sent it on; and finally, as on an unscheduled Christmas morning, it was in my hands. Oh happy day!

Baby's image is one of solidity. She projects an aura of uncompromising, unembellished *force*. The short, thick barrel. The imposing caliber. The dark, masterfully worked wood. The swelling magazine. The absence of the unessential. These combine into an impression that would be brutal if it were not so cleanly purposeful. One is reminded of Mr. Robert Wilson's "short, heavy, shockingly big-bored 505 Gibbs" in the Hemingway story. (On checking, I find it was "short, *ugly*, shockingly big-bored." But Baby is not ugly. Not to her father.)

The details of the ZKK action are very interesting. I had seen one before but had

Table 1:

FACTORY 458's

	Barrel	Magazine	Weight
Remington	24"	4	9
Winchester	26/22"	3	8½
Ruger	24"	3	9
Whitworth	24"	3	8
Mannlicher	26½"	4	9
Mark X	24"	3	8¼
Colt-Sauer	24"	3	10½
———————————————————————————————————————			
"Baby"	21"	5	11½

Table 2:

RECOIL COMPARISON
(g divided by 7,000 times mv)

Common Weight	Caliber	Bullet	R*
Group A	30-06	220	75
± 8½	375	300	107
	416	410	135
	458	500	148½
Group B	460 S (21")	500	161.4
± 10½	505 G	525	172
	500 J	535	183
	460 W	500	198
Group C	475 A&M	600	214
14+	600 N	900	244
	510 Wells	700	250

Divide this figure by the measured weight of the individual piece to reach comparative recoil effect, before modification by stock design.

not really examined it. It may be described as a "new-fashioned Mauser," with massive twin lugs, a very broad extractor claw, 90° rotation, and rear-mounted ejector. The "magnum" stroke is naturally long, but very smooth. There is no guide rib, but none seems necessary as the bolt is very accurately fitted, with little play even fully rearward and almost none in travel. The bolt stop is that of the Winchester 70. The safety rides conventionally on the right of the bolt head, rotating fore-and-aft. It is of the positive variety, locking striker and bolt while freeing the trigger—all very solidly arranged. *It works backwards*—"safe" forward and "fire" aft—labeled "safe" and "fire"—in English. One reflects that since no Communist can ever aspire to ownership of a rifle built on this action (What do you want with a hunting rifle, comrade?) the safety may be built backwards to help filthy capitalists (English-speaking) to get killed hunting lions. Every little bit helps.

The trigger is single-stage and breaks very cleanly at 42 ounces—two pounds ten—without creep or backlash. It is not a bench-rest trigger, but it is nearly perfect for its purpose.

The action frame seems to be an investment casting, but it is so well finished and fitted that it is hard to tell. The serial number—brace yourself—is seven *billion,* two hundred fifty-two million, five hundred four thousand, two hundred seven! It would appear that the Czechs have been equipping the Chinese, and for quite a spell at that. One hopes they put *all* the markings on in English.

The rear sight is both simple and ingenious. It is integral with the rear scope dovetail and spans the receiver bridge fore-and-aft. It is so designed as to be retracted downward out of the way when a scope is in place, and to spring up into line at the touch of a button on the starboard side. It does, too. However, it locks in the down position, and since I do not wish this to happen inadvertently I blocked out this feature. The eye-piece is fully adjustable, on the slide-and-clamp principle, but the locking screw heads are not hardened and are easy to deform if care is not used in tightening. This is a standard and exasperating feature of all the world's sights. Drilled out to ¼", the aperture is optically superb—very precise, very fast, and with almost no blockage of the forward view.

The rifle is 42" long, overall. This is the length of a Remington 742, or a Savage 99 C, or a Ruger 77 (short action). It's two inches shorter than most "magnums," and almost five inches shorter than a long-action Weatherby V. Inches may not be important, but Baby "feels short" with her 11½ pounds balanced between the palms. I specified 11½ pounds, loaded, and when I put five rounds in the magazine and placed the rifle on a scale, it read one-one-point-five-oh. Gratifying.

For ammunition I had a supply of Norma cases loaded with 500-grain Hornady's and 90 grains of #4064. The clock showed this combination to start very uniformly at 2,260 f/s, from 21". This seemed to call for a 150 yard zero, printing 1¾" high at one hundred and a bit over 5" low at 200. (Who ever heard of shooting anything dangerous—tanks excluded—at 200? All my authorities agree that you never take on anything tough at more than 40. Still, if I can get what amounts to line-of-sight impact all the way out to 175, why turn it down?)

As it turns out, Baby is great fun to shoot. The forward balance—just at the receiver ring—makes her very steady. The bright, square post is clear and sharp in the ghost ring. The trigger is most mannerly. On the break there is a satisfying baritone boom, accompanied by a vigorous but not vicious surge back into the shoulder. Bench-testing with Baby is not child's play, but position shooting is very pleasant. It is commonplace to hear that one should shoot a heavy only from offhand. Perhaps. I have not shot them all. But Baby is distinctly more comfortable from prone or sitting than a good many badly organized 30-caliber rifles I have met. The only thing I notice is a bit of soreness on the middle knuckle of the middle finger of my shooting hand, such as you may encounter when shooting a square-backed 44 Peacemaker, and a tender thumb if I leave it on the safety lever. (As I said, that safety arrangement is doubtless a commie conspiracy.) I shot 42 rounds on my first session, and I noticed no tenderness of shoulder or cheekbone next day.

Some gunmakers realize that the rear portion of the trigger guard, on any piece that kicks, should *not* be vertical. Note how the makers of fine shotguns have long inserted a slanting curve of steel at this point to deflect the second finger smoothly downward on recoil. This should be a standard feature of any "magnum" bolt action, but obviously it isn't—not on Winchester nor Remington nor Ruger nor Weatherby. And not on ZKK either. I intend to fit some sort of buffalo horn "adapter" to Baby as soon as I figure out a neat, strong way to do it.

Accuracy is eminently satisfying, though I will not elaborate upon it. An unconscionable amount of balderdash is written about rifle accuracy in the trade papers, and I do not wish to become a party to it. A mystique has grown up, evidently based on a sort of journalistic one-upmanship, which would have us believe that anything short of half-minute accuracy is unworthy of mention. In this editorial climate, to tell it as it is is to be scorned as a spastic, and the only way to praise a product is to lie about it. I do not choose to do this. I'm just going to admit that these half-inch sporting rifles are beyond my competence, my experience, and my appreciation, and let it go at that. Suffice to say that Baby is extremely accurate. My first three-shot test group at 100 yards measured 1¼" center-to-center, and I was delighted. If anyone regards this sort of performance as pedestrian he is welcome. For me it is superb. Not all my groups were that good, but once I got well and truly zeroed I left the bench (with an acknowledged touch of relief) and went to more interesting things.

Establishing to my own satisfaction that the piece was *very* powerful, *very* accurate, and surprisingly controllable, the next step was to work up a "manual of arms" that I could print on my reflexes, so that in action to come I could respond to stimuli without going into a conference with myself. Several things were involved: quick operation of the bolt, domination of the reversed safety, quick mounting of the rifle through 360°, "eyes-off" loading, and extremely intimate communion with this particular trigger.

The bolt came first. I have used a bolt-action rifle since before I found out about girls, but each action has its own characteristics. (And I never expect to find one as slick as that old Krag I started on.)

The bolt action is properly operated without removing the butt from the shoulder. A surprising number of younger shooters don't know this, having grown up in the era of the self-loader. The management of the bolt is simple enough, but it does need a bit of practice, and individualized practice with the particular action to be used. The index finger leaves the trigger instantly as the shot is fired, stabbing straight forward beneath the bolt knob and camming it upward with the first phalange. The bolt is retracted with the root of the index finger and thrust forward and down with the base of the thumb. The full stroke is no more than a flick, executed in a bit less than one second as the piece is returned to battery after recoil. One should not take the field with a bolt-action rifle until he has mastered this "bolt-flick."

I worked out the following drill, and I commend it to the enthusiast:

Turn on the evening news, and place yourself across the room from the tube, rifle across your knees, cocked and locked. (If you value your tube, best check for an empty chamber.) Place both hands in position, trigger finger outside the guard, thumb on safety. Now, whenever a written statement appears on the screen, check it for "O's." Quickly, mount the rifle, slip the safety and snap on as many O's as you can, flicking the bolt as necessary. The first O is easy, the second is harder, and the third can be a challenge, as they only leave that notice on for seconds. Remember to squeeze *carefully.* Aimless snapping is not the answer. I did this most evenings for more than a month before I took off for Africa, and I like to think it paid off. Bolt work became automatic and fast, and I got to be very reliable with that Peoples' Revolutionary Democratic safety. (Better luck next time, comrades.)

In live practice, I used Baby in three-second offhand singles, on the running double at 50 yards, and on the charging lion problem (a single five-second attempt at 75, followed by a two-second divergent option at half distance). I trained myself to keep that big magazine loaded by replacing singles, eyes-off, between stations. Baby performed flawlessly—not exactly light, but short, quick, and handy. Apparent recoil faded from considerable to negligible. I exploded large boulders and shot through large stumps. Baby *delivered.* "You want it, you got it!" It seemed that in both concept and execution we had created a superb artifact.

Nothing is perfect except in the mind of God, and Baby does have some features that I would change. Naturally I would prefer the safety to work the other way, but because of the way it locks the bolt handle, this would require a completely different design. I will attend to that vertical trigger guard in due course. Beyond that I would like a slightly longer fore-end and a Parkerized finish on the barrel—esthetic matters that another might not fancy. I would like the front sight mounted on a barrel band—it looks stronger that way. Lastly, the front plate of the magazine needs to be replaced in heavier gauge. As of now, with some eighty rounds fired, it is badly dented by the noses of reserve cartridges. A small point but still in need of attention.

No matter. Trivial imperfections can be ignored. The time came to put theory into practice, to press the issue "to its logical conclusion in unmitigated act"—in trial by battle.

We were ready. We went back to Africa.

The U.N.O., that ludicrous propaganda platform, would rather we didn't go hunting in Rhodesia, but it is in no position—yet—to give us orders, so we were able to arrange a splendid two-week shoot up in the Zambezi Valley between Kariba and Chirundu. It speaks volumes for the gallant people of Rhodesia that they could be so kind to visitors from a country whose official policy was dedicated to their destruction. Politics aside, we made the trip, and the hunting was marvelous.

Naturally I wanted to use Baby on big game, but really big game is not easy to organize. Rhino are *verboten*, though certainly not uncommon. Hippo are big enough but they call for specialized enterprise and localities. Elephant possibly, and buffalo certainly, were the targets. Our party of five was allotted three elephants—one duke and two barons. Zambezi elephants were tame as cattle at that time, and one could not bring home any ivory, so I passed. This did not promise much rifle testing, but as it turned out Baby did get into some very interesting action.

Preliminary conversation was something of a blow. At Kariba Airport I ran right into Terry, who had been with me on buffalo two years before when he recouped my failure with a 250-grain soft-point by way of a classic brain shot with his 470. I told him that I now had a proper weapon—a 460. He had heard of it.

"What think?"

"Bloody awful!"

"How so?"

"Shoots right through everything. Wastes all its power on the far side."

"Well, but I can use soft-points."

"Never use soft-points. Never! Bloody awful!"

Despite this inauspicious exchange I refused to be depressed. I had both solids and soft-points available, and besides full penetration is not all that bad if the channel is large and the placement is right. Like most experienced woodsmen, Terry was a dedicated conservative. Perhaps overly so.

Both Paul and Johnny, our two pros, agreed with Terry that soft-points in a heavy were only for lions, so I commenced operations with the 500-grain Hornady solids. Their jackets are of thick, mild steel—copper plated. They will draw a magnet, in case anyone doubts. They neither bend nor break up.

We drew blood on the morning of the second day. It was thus:

My partner was Dr. Albert Pauckner, of Ansbach, Germany, and our pro was Johnny Bunce, of the Rhodesian Department of Parks and Wildlife. His tracker was California, of the Matabele. Johnny packed his G.I. Winchester 70, in 458. Albert was using a scoped custom Mauser on a G-98 action, in 375. I, of course, had Baby.

We were truck-mounted and moving up a long, U-shaped valley which was covered with thin orchard bush and split by a meandering donga, varying from six to twelve feet in depth. From wall to wall the valley measured perhaps 500 yards. I saw my first klipspringer on its precipitous sides, bounding aloft like plump, gray chamois. Baboons were plentiful, and obviously annoyed by our rumbling Unimog.

Temporarily distracted from our main quest by the antics of these lesser people,

I did not spot the two bulls below on our port bow as the track led us up the westerly wall, but as the truck jammed to a halt Johnny's hissed alert was very authoritative.

Quickly over the side, the four of us bent low and plunged straight down the fall line toward the donga.

I had won the toss that morning. The first shot, if any, was to be mine.

The baboons were further excited by our behavior, and set up a shout.

The bottom of the donga contained a trickle of water, and its muddy bed left no doubt about the immediate presence of *Synceros.* We were very close aboard. Again, the smell. Again, the prickling of the scalp.

California led, and in less than 150 yards he indicated that the two bulls had to be just ahead, up over the lip of the donga. And we looked—and they were.

Making contact with buffalo in the wild may not impress some people, but for me it is a heart-stopping thrill. There they were—huge and black. Baby was in my hands. This was the moment!

They were much too far. Forty yards is maximum for dangerous game, and these were three times that. We had all slid up onto the rim of the donga in prone, and I expected Johnny to order us to slide quietly back down again, so we could try for a closer approach.

"Take him!" he whispered. "The one on the left is bigger."

"From here?"

"Yes, quickly! They're spooked by the baboons. They won't wait. Shoot!"

Well, O.K. The position is prone. The target is big. The range is something over a hundred. The problem is not marksmanship. It is tactics. You just don't pester buff that far away. But he says "Shoot!" O.K. Here goes!

The sharply squared gold post is bright against the black hide. I want it well forward —into bone. He checks his trot and turns sideways, staring back. Gently—press— gently—WHAM!

(Jim Wilkinson later asked me if shooting that big gun from prone wasn't something of a tooth-rattler. So help me, I never felt a thing! My mind was otherwise occupied.)

The bull pitched forward on his chest, got up and fell again, thrashing. We could not know it, but the ponderous bullet had whipped right through him, breaking *both* shoulders and clipping the top of the heart. Some power may have indeed been wasted, but Baby has it to waste.

At the shot the other bull whirled and trotted toward us, angling to the left. Albert's shot—a 300-grain solid, delivered quartering rearward just ahead of the shoulder —went home.

Nothing. No reaction at all.

What's wrong? Albert couldn't have missed—not from prone at 75 yards, on a target that size. The bull turned and ran, looking remarkably fit.

Everybody got up and leapt about, as is customary in Africa. I can't get used to it, as I have been brought up to lie low after shooting. But I followed the custom here.

"Kill that one!" shouted Johnny, pointing at mine, which was tossing his great horns and knocking down trees. I advanced to a clear spot, went to sitting and broke his neck. This shot was entirely unnecessary but we didn't know it at the time.

Albert, Johnny, and California had gone right after the second bull, which had stopped in a patch of thorn and was glaring back at them. They halted fifty yards out. I was to the right and a bit farther, perhaps eighty yards—but I was sitting down, rock solid.

"Here it comes," I thought. "He sees them. He's been hurt—Albert *must* have hit him—and now he'll charge, either with or before the shot. And I'll stop him! Point of the shoulder. That's what Baby is for."

Albert fired. Nothing! The bull, not having read the book, whirled and dived into the donga, reappearing beyond at a spanking trot, apparently untouched. He angled rapidly uphill to the right, opening the range as he neared a brushy saddle that afforded full concealment.

Problem! If he's wounded he must not get to cover. *Is* he wounded? He must be! Albert is a good shot—you don't qualify for a German *Jagdschein* unless you can shoot—and a 375 is much gun. But on he runs. Neither Albert nor Johnny shoots. *He's getting away.* If he gets to that saddle we're in for it. Somebody may be killed. Shoot!

Now the excellent sights and superior trajectory of the custom rifle became significant. The "ghost ring" did not obscure the target as express sights would have, and I had no need to correct for range, even way out there. He's running now—remember to follow through—*careful*—WHAM!

On his nose, stone dead. Wow!

I opened the bolt, put the empty in my pocket, replaced two of the long, fat cartridges in the magazine and one in the chamber, closed the bolt, pressed the safety forward to lock the action, and stood up.

It was over. I caressed Baby lovingly. A warm feeling of confidence and serenity seemed to flow from the superb instrument into my hands and arms, and on up to my head. Wow!

Post morta followed.

The first bull had been hit exactly on the point of the shoulder, as intended, and I placed an empty in the hole to help the illustration. He was not "iced"—only a brain shot will do that to a buffalo—but he was totalled in his tracks. We found no bullet, of course.

Both of Albert's shots had also gone right where he meant them to, the first quartering through the boiler room to exit the rib cage beyond, and the second right in the gozzle from dead ahead. The 375 is a formidable cartridge, with an unmatched record, but after examining his bull's wounds Albert looked long at his rifle and finally muttered, almost to himself, "I have no confidence in this gun."

No one knocks the 375, prince of the medium calibers, but Albert had shot perfectly, twice, and yet that bull would have had plenty of time and room to kill him if it had chosen to do so! When my 350 RM delivered only a flesh wound to a buffalo two years before, I assumed that it was because I had not used a solid, yet Albert had used solids—and in a more potent cartridge—and hit his animal better both times. I recalled that some of my South African friends had told me that shooting a buff with a medium is like shooting a man with a 38. It *may* suffice, and then again. . . .

The range on my first shot was 117 paces, and my legs are long. The terminal shot on Albert's bull was stepped off at exactly 175. That's too far, but, as with Elmer's famous deer, he was getting away. This hit, too, was a shoulder shot—a couple of inches higher and farther forward than that which dropped the first bull. All the 460 bullets were lost to "over penetration." The end-on 375 was recovered, unmarked except for rifling grooves. It, at any rate, had wasted no power beyond the target.

All in all, it was an intensely interesting episode, and Baby came through with flying colors.

By a series of lucky coincidences, my field testing was not terminated by that one encounter. Albert's bull turned out to be a freak, with only one horn which was all we could see until after he had been hit. The Game Department very courteously granted him another bull, and since he had expressed himself about the 375 I was glad to loan him Baby so that she could log some more missions. She logged them, and they were a bit weird.

Having established that the fine Hornady solids performed as expected, we wanted a chance to investigate the soft-points. I had a number of specially constructed 550-grain "inner belted" expanders built for me by a friend and loaded ahead of 89 grains of #4064. It was suggested that we load one such "up the spout" but fill the big magazine with five solids as a back-up. Thus prepared, Albert and Johnny sallied forth a couple of days later. I was not along, so what follows is hearsay.

By this time all of us had tagged-out on buff, except Albert, and the heads were good-to-average. It remained to bag a really impressive *nyati*, not that the smallish ones are not impressive enough as it is.

Albert and Johnny ran quickly on to a bunch of very big bulls. He picked a good one and smacked him solidly in the center of the shoulder, from offhand, with the 550 soft-point, at some thirty paces. The buff flinched at the tremendous blow but did nothing more. At this point a really enormous bull, which had been standing behind the first, swung round and looked at Albert over the neck of Number One.

Now what? We had all been strongly cautioned never to shoot at two buff in column, to avoid wounding the rearward beast with a spent bullet which might exit from the one in front. But here we had a problem. The front one had already been hit. He had not dropped. It was an apparent choice of one-away-wounded, certainly, against one-down-and-one-away-wounded, possibly.

"Shoot!" said Johnny. Albert flicked the bolt, bringing a solid under the pin, and shot. . . .

Both bulls fell in their tracks. Baby had killed two trophy buffalo (45″ and 48″) stone dead with one shot. (Wow!)

As it turned out the soft-point had ruptured completely in the massive shoulder bones of the near bull, delivering a temporarily paralyzing wound without reaching the vitals. The solid landed almost on top of the soft-point, drove straight through, exited, and took the second bull lengthwise, entering the center of the chest and lodging in the pelvis. Overpenetration? Yes, indeed! Unnecessary, but comforting withal.

Albert drew one of the elephant barons and naturally took Baby along for the dark deed. There was not much to finding elephants in the Zambezi Valley in 1977 (as a matter of fact we had some little trouble avoiding those we did not want), but the exigencies of communist invasion limited our leisure for trophy selection. Paul therefore led Albert right up to a medium-sized bachelor bull, about 45 pounds on each side, and they confronted each other in the thorn at all of twelve paces. As Peter Capstick puts it, a man who is not afraid of elephants has either never met a wild one up close or his wires are not properly connected. Nobody panicked, but everyone involved was—shall we say—a touch edgy. Albert's shot was well centered in deflection but too low. Instead of "the third wrinkle" it caught maybe the eighth. Amazingly, the bull's hind legs collapsed as if he had been driven back on his haunches. Obviously nothing a man can hold in his hands can drive 12,000 pounds backwards, but it looked as if Baby did.

Albert flicked the bolt at this point, but, not being in practice, he did not retract it all the way and thus closed it on the empty chamber. Obviously that could have been serious. But Paul was at his shoulder and fired with his 470 as the bull heaved sideways. Most probably the ball was over with that first shot, but we will never know.

(Moral: Select the rifle you intend to use, and practice with it until your hands work it without thought. This is not a minor consideration.)

This, then, will do for a field test. It holds no great surprises but it does tend to verify the utility of the concept. Six shots were fired, bagging four buffalo and one elephant. One shot on buffalo was unnecessary, one was free (though still very informative), and one was unsuccessful due to bullet construction. One feeding failure occurred, attributable to lack of personal practice.

I find no major fault with the weapon, though a couple of details in her design might be improved. I find her weight to be a distinct advantage in shooting, and not uncomfortable after two weeks of prowling the bush. I feel that Baby is indeed superior to any "stock" rifle now available for her task, but since that task is almost a thing of the past, I do not see her as a prototype for future standardization. However, if anyone wants to duplicate this piece, or to improve upon it, he is welcome, and I think the effort will afford him great pleasure and satisfaction.

Baby may be the end product of one specialized line of instrumental evolution. I devoutly hope that she may see action again, but, whether or not this is possible, she will hang on the wall henceforth as a heartening and wonderfully enduring testimony to the ideal of excellence. It's nice to know just how good things can get.

23

Rhodesian
Elegy

I CAME BACK FROM RHODESIA filled with excitement, enthusiasm, and tension. The excitement was caused by the marvelous countryside—wild, wide and beautiful. The enthusiasm was for the wonderful people I met there, and their warm hospitality extended to a citizen of a nation whose policy toward theirs was best described as befuddled bullying. And the tension, of course, was due to the peril that faced that embattled outpost of European Civilization—a peril well-met at that time, but little noticed by those who were not actually on the scene. As is not unusual historically, here was a situation in which general catastrophe was being fended off by a handful, while those they defended ate, drank, and made merry, unaware of what was at stake.

It is dreadfully frustrating to speak on this subject. When a couple of my Rhodesian friends asked me what Americans thought of their struggle, I could only answer sheepishly that the generality of Americans not only didn't know about their struggle, they didn't even know what sort of a country Rhodesia was. They absolutely did not know that America's future was directly dependent upon that of Rhodesia. Most Americans know—now—about Arabian oil. Few know—yet—about Rhodesian chromium. But the simple fact is that one cannot make modern weapons without steel; one cannot make high-quality steel without chromium; and when Rhodesia fell all of the known chromium sources on the planet fell into the hands of powers inimical to

the West. In this sense, the frontier of the civilization of which the United States is a part lay on the Zambezi River.

Rhodesia was an oval-shaped, independent republic in the heart of Southern Africa, landlocked between the Limpopo River on the south and the Zambezi on the north. In the days of empire it was known as Southern Rhodesia, since what is now known as Zambia was then Northern Rhodesia. It was the size of California, and lay about as far south of the equator as the Valley of Mexico lies to the north. It was an open land of big distances, but almost entirely wooded, without any true desert. Its highlands reached 8,500 feet on its eastern frontier with Mozambique, and its lowlands formed the Zambezi trench on the north. Its southern border with the Republic of South Africa was open and friendly. To the southwest lay Botswana, at present reasonably secure. But northwest, north, and east there was danger. The president of Zambia wanted to invade, and with the 1974 coup in Portugal, Mozambique changed from a disordered guerrilla territory into an organized enemy state, directed from the Chicom base at Dar-es-Salaam. So Rhodesia at that time formed a salient of civilization extending into and bordered on three sides by chaos. It lived by skill, courage, and good cheer reminiscent of the vanished Britain of 1940. It menaced no one, and it asked only to be let alone to work out its own destiny.

Rhodesia was a new nation, founded by Cecil Rhodes in 1890. It had been inhabited since pre-history by a succession of little-known peoples including that vanished race which built the curious stone city of Zimbabwe in the eighth century. Its current Bantu population is mainly Mashona and Matabele, who entered the land in the fourteenth and nineteenth centuries respectively, and who are traditional enemies. The Matabele would almost surely have achieved their purpose of exterminating the Mashona if the Europeans had not appeared on the scene. These Europeans were of British stock (with a prominent Scottish element) and Rhodesia in 1977 was an English-speaking nation. Unlike most other colonial offshoots of England, it was settled more by winners than losers, and this resulted in a society composed mainly of what an educationalist would call "high-achievers." (Standardized I.Q. tests rated Rhodesian children some 10% above the norm for English-speaking children, worldwide.) The total European population was about a quarter of a million, while the Bantu people numbered some 5½ million, making Rhodesia one of the smallest nations in the world. The "Europeans" paid 97½% of the taxes, though they owned only about 50% of the land.

The common journalistic term for the Rhodesian regime was "white minority," the implication being that 250,000 white Rhodesians held several million black Rhodesians in some sort of forcible subjugation. The facts of this matter were rather otherwise, but seldom aired abroad. In Rhodesia skin color was not considered in voting procedures. One might vote if he (1) had a high-school education or equivalent, (2) owned a small amount of real property, or (3) earned a very modest income. (Schooling was free and public.) Such limitations on the franchise are denounced in some circles in terms that would be ludicrous if they were not taken so seriously. It is true that the white population outvoted the black by a large ratio, but if this constituted subjugation it must certainly be termed an optional subjugation, comparable to that in a well-run household in which everybody is expected to wash up before coming to the dinner table.

What obtained then, in Rhodesia, was a developing "western" nation, complete with modern conveniences, inheriting British traditions and lifestyles, superimposed upon a Bantu tribal region which contained both educated, twentieth-century blacks and a large number of what used to be called aborigines. The government was trying to promote a system of bi-cultural evolution which could bring the tribesmen into modern times without destroying the nation that five generations of white pioneers had carved out of the wilderness. To the degree that they succeeded they were abhorred by the black African states to the north, who have pretty thoroughly demonstrated that *they* cannot do this. Those innocents who are not faced with these problems may chant "One man, one vote" like Orwell's sheep, but one cannot but wonder what they would say if this meant, *literally,* giving Manhattan back to the Indians.

That is exactly what Britain told the Rhodesians to do, some ten years back. The Rhodesian response was something like "Thanks, but no thanks." Britain insisted. The result, on 11 November, 1965, was the Unilateral Declaration of Independence (U.D.I.) and the birth of a nation. (It is interesting that Ian Smith had been a Spitfire pilot in WW II, whereas his opposite number, Harold Wilson, had been a "conscientious objector."

This U.D.I. made Rhodesia a "non-nation" in most chancelleries, since it is easy to be high-handed with a very small country. For the United States of America to anathematize an ex-British colony for declaring itself independent of Britain—unilaterally— was, to put it mildly, peculiar. Evidently the Rhodesians took our example all too literally.

When we asked our State Department about this oddity they offered a triple ploy. First they said that Rhodesia, while following our own rebel example, was in rebellion against *Britain,* who is now our staunch ally. (Did you notice how staunchly Britain came to our aid in Viet Nam? Rhodesia, on the other hand, offered a battalion.)

If you cast that foolishness aside, the second response was that *Rhodesia did not practice majority rule.* (They really had a hard time saying this with a straight face.) If the U.S. associated only with majority-rule regimes we would be down to about 20 out of the world's 140-odd sovereign states. And even if we did hold that the one-man one-vote principle was the absolute be-all and end-all of political morality, we are formally committed to the policy that we do *not* interfere with other people's internal affairs.

Pressed further, State finally came out with it. We must at all costs balance the Third World against the Soviet Bloc in the United Nations. The Third World (Arabs and black African states) looks upon Southern Africa with what can only be described as a psychotic frenzy. The official word is "Get Whitey! Reason, justice, and even self-interest have nothing to do with the case. He who is not for us is against us, and we number scores of millions, against a besieged outpost of 250,000. Get Whitey!"

So the U.S., as a nation, felt that it must excoriate a tiny and absolutely unaggressive group of people who would like to have been our friends, while at the same time it grovelled diplomatically before huge and alien power masses who are our declared and dedicated enemies. There is a word for that, but it sticks in the throat of one who had thought better of his country.

So much, however, for the morals of the case. Outside pressure finally destroyed Rhodesia.

In the words of Ian Smith, Prime Minister:

> "We believe in evolutionary change, not revolution. More than 50 years ago Rhodesians chose the course of responsible government.
>
> "From that time on it has always been accepted that Rhodesia was the home of all its peoples and was shared equitably between them.
>
> "With the passage of time, this philosophy has been more and more firmly entrenched with complete justification.
>
> "We have no other home, we have no other country. We are white Rhodesians and, in a more general term, white Africans, and have just as much right to our position here as have our fellow black Rhodesians.
>
> "I have never heard a contrary argument and if there is one I would like to know what it is.
>
> "If anyone believes that such people are going to allow themselves to be pushed around in their own country then they are out of their minds."

These are not the words of an unreasonable man, nor of a political innocent, nor of a racist, nor of a coward.

Inside Rhodesia at that time the mood—insofar as I could assess it on a short visit—was tense but cheerful. Nothing unites nor enlivens like the threat of a common enemy, and morale, especially in the armed forces, was superb. Black and white Rhodesians served side by side in the army, and they knew absolutely what they were fighting for. From Zambia and from Mozambique invaders came in small bands by night. They called themselves "Freedom Fighters," but the term was hard to explain to those—predominantly black—whom they murdered. Certainly they did not persuade the Shona troopers in the Rhodesian African Rifles, with whom I spent a day up on the frontier. The most solid of all military motives is the defense of one's soil, and that is what the Rhodesian war was about. "They come into our country without the right. They kill our people. They kill our cattle. They steal our food. So we kill them. We always win."

Eventually they lost, but they were never beaten.

It was inspiring to note how many "new" Rhodesians I met—those who had immigrated since U.D.I. They came from elsewhere (I met a couple of expatriate U.S. marines), in search of a clean frontier atmosphere, free from smog, strikes, hippies, drugs, generation gaps, pornography, street crime, and unisex. And they found it. The price was hard work, duty, and danger. Nearly every adult male, and many women, were in some branch of the security forces, regular or reserve. To defend a border 1,000 miles long with Rhodesia's population left no room for non-combatants. This was just as well, for it attracted the strong while scaring off the weak. As Burnham said, "Men who are looking for a safe thing should keep away from Africa!"

And Rhodesians were traditionally strong. The pioneers of the 90's fought hard for their land against both nature and hostile tribesmen. The legends of the Shangani and Mazoe patrols were well known, and "Southern Rhodesians" fought in both the Boer War and WW I. In WW II some 15% of Rhodesia's white population signed up for military service, and about one in ten died on duty. Only a Rhodesian team ever made a clean sweep of the Commonwealth marksmanship championships at Bisley. (Small wonder that this nation chose a fighter pilot for its first prime minister.)

(In a revealing incident one recent immigrant was a German—a specialist in auto maintenance and repair who brought not only his family but most of the associates in his shop. He said that since European television kept insisting that Rhodesia was such a terrible place, it must really be great. So much for media credibility.)

Well, Rhodesia was lost. Along with Cuba, Nicaragua, El Salvador, Iran, Angola, Mozambique, Cambodia, and Viet Nam—among others. In 1945 we held the world in our hand, and we let it drop. May God forgive us, for our posterity will not.

24

Kriegsoberst!

CONSIDERED IN THE MASS, the human race is somewhat depressing. But what makes it worth God's trouble (and our amazement) is that occasionally it produces magnificent individuals. What these individuals have done staggers the imagination, and serves forever as an example for the very best human beings to emulate.

These are the heroes. Magnificence can be achieved outside of conflict—witness Leonardo, Shakespeare, Beethoven—but mainly the heroes are warriors, because valor finds its most natural expression in war, and valor is a very wonderful thing.

One might be forgiven for feeling that the time of the mighty warrior is past—that individual splendor no longer matters in the modern world—but he would be wrong. I submit, and I will attempt to establish that *the greatest warrior of all times was born in 1916, and is alive as I write.* The quality of greatness is obviously subjective, and depends to some extent upon one's viewpoint, but, if you can believe what you are about to read, I think you will have no choice but to accept my astounding claim.

Hans-Ulrich Rudel, Colonel, Luftwaffe, Retired, was a military aviator. He flew various aircraft, but his specialty was the Junkers 87, a single-engined, two-place, ground-attack machine which was designed as a dive-bomber and served that purpose well, though it was to fly another sort of mission into history at Rudel's hands.

This was the "Stuka" (*Sturz-Kampf-Bomber*), the crank-winged mainstay of the German close-air-support arsenal.

Somewhat dated even as WW II began, it flew neither very fast nor very far nor very high, for essentially it was a "mule"—strong, tough, enduring, uncomplicated, stable in the air—and in the hands of a flying genius it became the most fearful tank destroyer ever devised. Rudel flew the Stuka as a dive bomber until 1943, and with it sank the Russian battleship Marat with one 2,200-pound AP bomb—a mighty feat of arms—but his role as panzer-killer did not develop fully until he began to fly "Gustav" (Ju 87 G) which carried a 37mm anti-tank gun under each wing. *With this weapon he destroyed five-hundred nineteen Russian armored vehicles* (tanks and assault guns). These are those positively confirmed—the true tally is higher. Five-hundred nineteen tanks. One at a pass. Single-handed. That's about three armored divisions—wrecked by one man. The tank is today's dragon. How many dragons did St. George kill?

Rudel flew 2,530 combat missions, on every one of which he was in distinct danger of death. He was shot down more than thirty times—always from the ground, though he was often hit from the air. He was wounded so often that it was unusual for him to fly unbandaged. As the end approached he was in the air before first light, expending his ammunition, landing, rearming, taking off again to repeat the attack as long as there was light to shoot by. As his aircraft was chewed to unserviceability by ground fire he nursed it back to base where a fresh one was warmed up and ready. The only breaks occurred when he was shot down and had to make his way home on the ground.

Courage, steadfastness, endurance, devotion to duty. These are the classic virtues of the soldier. But they do not fully encompass Rudel. His crowning element was *skill*—of a sort such as to be beyond normal comprehension. The Gustav could not reveal its presence to its prey without being shot to pieces by the light automatic cannon with which the Russians protected their armor, with increasing effectiveness as they acquired experience. The Gustav test squadron envisioned the attack's being delivered too far out and too high, at a slant range of 400 meters. Those who tried this against live targets did not last long. Rudel reset his guns to converge at 100 meters, and came in by choice about 15 meters off the ground. He attacked at full throttle, flaps up—at a bit over 200 m/h. At this rate just two seconds elapsed between the firing point and the target. If the target blew up, as it usually did, it was necessary to dodge violently to avoid running straight into the explosion!

Consider this: First you locate your target concentration with some accuracy—you cannot grope for it without getting shot. Then you assume your preferred attack line and drop to tree-top level. You can't see your tanks yet but you commence to "jink" violently, weaving to the attack like a weasel. Then suddenly you *can* see them. Of several you must pick one that is headed properly—your 37's cannot bust a Russian tank from front or rear and you must try for the thin side skin behind which the ammunition is stored. You have one second to level your airplane, align the reflector sight, and squeeze the trigger on your stick. At 200 m/h and less than 50 feet you must dip the nose slightly as you aim—the guns are set level with the horizontal axis of

your ship—an instant's delay and you're in the ground. Both guns fire together, the two shots converging one football field's length in front of your nose. They are fully automatic but of slow cyclic rate. At this distance those two rounds are all you get. You cannot wait to see if you have hit, because if you have and you don't bank instantly you'll blow yourself up. In your five-G bank, wing-tip scraping the shrubbery, you feel a violent shock as the blast wave hits you. Scratch one dragon! There are thousands more.

That's a good trick! It is so good that it is, for practical purposes, impossible. That is why Rudel achieved 500 plus kills with it while the number-two man in the league logged 60. I would rate that feat about the same as placing a snap shot with a rifle, in the head, on a running target, at 100 paces. A very good man might bring it off once in a while. Rudel did it with the regularity of a printing press. *On his last attack he did it with stick only, both legs having been disabled.*

It is easy to say that Rudel was very lucky. Obviously a man who was so often seriously damaged without being killed is lucky. But the fact that in 2,530 missions he was hit as seldom as he was attests to much more than mere chance. If a man plays golf twice a day and holes-out in one most of the time we can hardly attribute that to luck.

It is fitting that a legendary warrior should be honored with a unique award, and thus it was. As the incredible tale unfolded Hitler decreed that one special medal be created especially for this one man. Twenty-seven Germans, including such notables as Rommel, Hartmann, Dietrich, Galland, and von Strachwitz, were awarded the Knight's Cross of the Iron Cross with swords and diamonds. For Rudel it was the Knight's Cross with swords, diamonds, and golden oak leaves—the only one of its kind. (At the behest of his advisors Hitler had twelve such medals struck, eleven to be held for future heroes of stature equal to that of the first recipient. No such man ever turned up, and the whereabouts of the eleven are now unknown. (Rudel has seen a swords-and-diamonds—without oak leaves—in the U.S. but he thinks it is a replica.)

When I began teaching in Europe five years ago I asked about the whereabouts and condition of the colonel. I first heard that he had died of a stroke in '70 and assumed that to be the end of the story. A couple of years later I discovered that the stroke, though paralytic, had not proved fatal. New enquiries were initiated and it turned out that Rudel is hard to meet only in that he travels a great deal and schedules often conflict.

My interest is predominantly in weaponry. While I can take off and land certain airplanes I am certainly no aviator. But even for an expert pilot Rudel is something very special. To play the piano in the band is one thing. To be a Rubinstein or a Cliburn is another. Still, the Gustav was a *weapon*. It called for very special handling and it fascinated me. It is the earliest ancestor of today's A-10, which may or may not prove to be a satisfactory answer to the new wave of communist tanks. Gustav, without Rudel, was a marginal device. With Rudel it was a landmark in the history of weapons, and very pertinent to my researches into the history of marksmanship.

A meeting was arranged, and took place in Sonnthofen, Bavaria, in August of 1978. Once a legend is launched, all sorts of anecdotes accrue, and it was my purpose to determine the absolutely straight story, free from intermediaries and translations. I had read *Stuka Pilot*, the English-language rendition of the autobiographical *Trotzdem*, but there were details that remained unclear. Here was the chance to set the record straight before it became too late for either or both of us.

Colonel Rudel is a solid, compact man, about 5'8". His hair is now gray-white, but the large head and straight, prominent nose are recognizable from earlier photos. The stroke hit the right side, on which he lost his lower leg in action, so he moves with some difficulty. Under the circumstances it is remarkable that he walks at all. His hands—perhaps the deadliest hands ever seen—are short-fingered and broad. His manner is quite courteous and accommodating, especially in view of how constantly he must answer the same questions, but the explosive forcefulness of character for which he is famous is still apparent. It is an awesome sensation to sit and converse with a living titan.

Since time was short we got quickly to details. He speaks a little English and I a little German. We both speak passable Spanish. Additionally we had the help of the charming Frau Rudel, his third wife, and of Walter Luger, a student of mine from Salzburg who is fluent in English. Thus what follows is not garbled in translation.

The exact technique of Gustav's attack, as described earlier, was first discussed. The characteristics of the gun were noted: It was derived from the 3.7cm "Flak" anti-aircraft cannon rather than the infantry anti-tank gun of the same caliber. It weighed about 2,500 pounds as installed, and fired a one-kilo AP projectile with a core of tungsten carbide at a velocity of 3,400 f/s. *Each gun carried a clip of just six rounds.* This was no garden hose, but rather a sniper's weapon. Without "zero-tolerance" precision in handling it was useless. Naturally the installation hampered the Stuka's performance, but the mule didn't mind overmuch. The guns did prohibit dive bombing, but Gustav carried no bombs.

In the Luftwaffe, many of whose fighter pilots scored kills in the hundreds, Rudel's air-to-air record was soberly tallied at eleven. Eleven Russian fighters shot out of the air with the mule! How many with the "single-shot" cannon? Five. Granting a surfeit of opportunity, this is still superhuman marksmanship, something like stopping a lion's charge with a pistol.

Which was more astounding, the flying or the shooting? On at least one occasion Rudel flew his pursuer into the ground, without firing a shot. A very important Russian, with many credit badges on his Lagg 5, popped his flaps to get in close and nearly did the job with his center-line cannon. Rudel pulled him into a decreasing-radius vertical bank until, trying to cross the chord, the Lagg lost it and fell on one wing.

Additionally, it was a Rudel specialty to land his mule in the mud behind Russian lines to pick up downed German flyers. He would trust no one else with this task.

Curious about a particular exploit that suggested John Colter's run for life from the Blackfeet, I put a question:

"On the occasion that you landed across the Dniester to rescue two comrades,

. . . and your aircraft stuck in the mud, preventing your take-off,

. . . and you made your way to the ice-clogged river,

. . . and stripped and swam 500 meters in the deadly cold water, losing a man on the way,

 . . . and, without clothing or shoes, you ran into a Russian patrol, which opened fire,

 . . . and you outran the Russians, barefoot, with a bullet through your shoulder,

 . . . and you then made it some 60 kilometers to the German position,

On that occasion, how long were you a casualty?"

The answer: "I was in aid station one day. The next day I killed ten tanks. Two days later I got eighteen. My feet were very painful, but I did not need to walk."

Another question: "You seem always to have carried a 6.35mm auto pistol (25 ACP) as a sidearm. How was it that you put your trust in so trifling a weapon?"

Answer: "Because I have never been a pessimist." (*That*, I must remember.)

Yet another: "Was it possible to over-stress the Ju 87?"

Answer: "No. Not as a dive bomber. You could not dive the Gustav, but without the guns the Stuka could be pointed straight down at full throttle without dive brakes and pulled out without creaking. Terminal velocity was about 600 K's."

When one expects too much he can be disappointed, but Rudel, unbelievable as it may sound, comes on "larger than life." His straightforward answers pile amazement until one sits bemused, pondering upon the apparently infinite capability of the human animal to surpass all sensible limits. It's an inspiring experience.

What does it take to be a hero? Very little if you use the word carelessly. There are football heroes, and cinema heroes, and heroes in novels, and "Heroes of the Soviet Union" (addressed socially, as *"Geroye"*). But what does it take to be a *real* hero? If we use Rudel as a model, it takes these things:

(a) A rugged, powerful body, inured to hardship and resistant to fatigue.

(b) Profound and unshakeable dedication to one's cause, together with sublime devotion to duty.

(c) Bravery so spectacular as to be called foolhardy by those who can't match it.

(d) Skill of an order so high as to be off the scales by which such things are normally measured.

A.   Rudel was from youth a physical culture fanatic. Every sport attracted him, but especially those calling for endurance and hard conditioning. He neither drinks nor smokes—instead he runs, swims, and skis—even now. He started with excellent genes and built upon them a tireless, rock-hard body.

B.   Rudel is the son of a Methodist minister, and regards Communism as the doctrine of the Devil—a dire succubus that is devouring both Christianity and Western Civilization at one sitting. To him the war was a crusade, and to tear into the endless Eastern hordes was both a holy obligation and a joy. As a German, he took pride in the Germany that Hitler built, and, if he did not approve of Hitler's paganism*, he could live with it as the best means of combatting the world enemy.

C.   Rudel's awesome physical courage needs no further elucidation. Bravery may not be uncommon, but it is always glorious. (And here I go against the popular

---

*Colonel Rudel comments: "Hitler was a deeply religious man." I don't know how to analyze that.

view that "moral courage" is somehow superior to physical. Moral courage is for politicians and philosophers. Physical courage is another thing entirely. As Buckley puts it, "If death or torture are not involved we should use some other word.")

D. Rudel's fantastic skill has been described, at least in a limited way. He may be the greatest flyer who ever flew an airplane, and, at the same time, the finest shot who ever fired a gun. This in one man!

Obviously these are extravagant claims, but let who will dispute them. We look forward to the tale.

In the Imperial War Museum in Vienna there is a Hall of Fame, wherein marble statues of the great men of old are displayed. There, among the various dukes and field marshals and princes and generals, I encountered the title "K.O." Being spotty in medieval European history I had to ask what this meant. The answer—"Kriegsoberst." Now *oberst* means "highest," and has come to be the military equivalent of "colonel" in English. But *Kriegsoberst* is altogether grander. "Krieg" means "war" in German, and "Kriegsoberst" is an antique term meaning "highest in war." It is not a military title but rather an honorific address, something like "highness" or "magnificence." It cannot be earned administratively—it must be accepted by consensus. I first heard Rudel thus titled in 1978, not in Germany but in Austria. Neither he nor his wife professed awareness of this development.* I think it fits beautifully. In official records he is listed as *Oberst, Luftwaffe, Ausser Dienst* (retired), but I think he should go down in history as *Kriegsoberst*, the man to remember.

I certify that I have read the foregoing material and that, while I may not agree with all of the opinions expressed therein, the facts are correct as per my notation.

_____

(1 November 1978)

Date

_____

Hans-Ulrich Rudel

---

*Colonel Rudel comments: "I have never been addressed as 'Kriegsoberst'—only as 'Oberst'." I would like to change that.

FireWorks

186

25

Wegener

TERRORISM MAY BE DEFINED as the indiscriminate employment of fear, principally against the innocent and uninvolved, in the pursuit of a debatable political point. It is by no means unique to our times, but it has suddenly become a matter of general concern because of the juxtaposition of modern weaponry upon general civil cowardice. Without firearms and explosives it is difficult to carry out, but without submission it is impossible.

Plain banditry is certainly wicked, and is dealt with harshly by sensible people, but it is relieved by a certain straightforward honesty. "I want what you have, so give it to me or I will kill you!" says the robber. This is evil, but we can meet it fairly. However, to say, "You must do what I want or I will kill this defenseless other person," is to announce that you have no decency, and that you count upon the decency of others to effect their undoing. This is to pervert and corrupt the very essence of righteousness, and is thus insufferable. In obscene parody, it is at once horrible and ridiculous. Unless it is mercilessly stamped out, just as piracy on the high seas was mercilessly stamped out, civilization will become both unworkable and dishonorable.

Queer as it may seem, there are those who actually try to justify terrorism. They claim that it is the weapon of the weak against the strong, and maintain that it is a legitimate act of war. This is ideological solecism, and to give it a moment's credence is a sin in itself. If one has a grievance his target is its author. To strike at a third party in order to coerce your adversary is worse than criminal—it is foul. The terrorist thus places himself outside of any considerations of respect or pity. He is worthy of all the mercy we afford the rabies virus.

In general, the will to act is what respectable society lacks. In general, we wring our hands and whimper. But not, however, *all* of us. Good men, worldwide, are growing angry. And with the anger may come the will. The hard line is indeed unfashionable at this time—at least in the Western World. But the case is still not hopeless. Certain groups are now organized to take suitable action against this hideous social chancre.

Pre-eminent among these is *Grenzschutzgruppe 9*, the special commando of the German border patrol, conceived at the Munich Olympic Games disaster of 1972, and consecrated at Mogadiscio in 1977. This unit is now fully prepared and fully tested in action—a bright, sharp, and finely tempered sword ready for use wherever the *Bundesrepublikdeutschland* may send it.

I first met GSG 9 and its distinguished commander, Ulrich Wegener, in 1974 when it was just begun. The matter of pistol training was discussed, and my opinion was that such an organization probably had little use for handguns since its missions would always be tactically offensive and thus pose scant need for personal defensive armament. In this I was wrong, for counter-terror tactics can include what might be termed the "Orang-attack," calling for such violent and athletic movements (down ropes, through windows, roof-to-roof, etc.) as almost to prohibit the carrying of a proper weapon of offense. Four members of the commando did attend one of my overseas sessions, but much water has run under the bridge since then and there is now a good deal of new shooting theory to sort out. Shooting is not the primary business of GSG 9, but its people must be able to shoot better than most if the occasion arises, as it has in the past and will again.

Currently staffed with 180 men, GSG 9 is a small unit. It must be, for its targets are pinpoints and it is very, very elite. One of its officers told me in '74 that he did not think the Table of Organization would ever be filled because he didn't think there were 180 men around who could measure up. Start with an advanced academic degree, medal-out in the Olympic trials, qualify in several languages, check out in flying, mountaineering, power swimming, hand-to-hand, and driving, and you may be considered—assuming your attitude and general appearance are superior. This is a veritable troop leader's dream!

Counter-terror is a very modern discipline, and its doctrine is still formulative. In Colonel Wegener GSG 9 has an ideal leader, for he is a quick-minded, inquisitive, scholarly man—brilliantly pioneering in his new field. On this last occasion I set out to interview him about his spectacular success at Mogadiscio, and he wound up interviewing me about combat shooting. There were certain technical failures at Mogadiscio, and Wegener is not a man to let such matters drop.

Astonishing as it may appear, the men of GSG 9 carry the pistol of their choice. This policy is less likely all the time now in the U.S. and practically unthinkable in Europe.

But the Colonel said, "Confidence in one's weapon is the big thing." (Where have we heard *that* before?) And the golden boys are given a free hand.

Naturally this is not the perfect answer in every case. At Mogadiscio the first man to confront the head goblin in the cockpit doorway was carrying a 38 Chief. He neatly placed all five rounds in the man's mid-section. Nothing happened. (Hardly to my surprise.) The grenade that was thrown in response was a Russian flash bomb, and the fact that it killed no one was due to its own inferior quality rather than expert defensive weaponry. Colonel Wegener pointed out that he was following a ministerial directive stipulating Geneva Convention ammunition. (Will politicians *never* learn to leave tactical matters to tacticians!) He has had that directive rescinded, but several people who were in that airplane are very lucky to be alive. There are things you can load into a Chief that will probably do much better, but a Chief is still not the right tool for that job.

What is? That's a good question, and we considered it. If *you* had to dive through a smoking, two-foot hole into the dark, expecting to confront several heavily-armed maniacs in a crowd of terrified non-combatants, what would *you* pick? The impact ballistics of smallarms are something of a specialty with me but I certainly do not have all the answers. The lads I met later on the range were sporting a variety of frangible-projectile ammunition for their sidearms, but you can only get so much out of a given combination of mass and velocity, and in the case of small-caliber pistol cartridges this does not seem to be enough.

Pistolcraft aside, I was especially interested in certain details of the two big strikes—Entebbe and Mogadiscio. It is not widely known that Wegener was invited by the Israelis to observe at Entebbe, but he was indeed there. He also was slightly wounded by—of all things—a bayonet. (I guess it was lucky that he was not bitten by a snake, everything considered.)

I had assumed that Colonel Netanyahu, the Israeli battalion commander who was killed, was hit by a 9mm Uzi bullet—because of his gradual response. As it happened he was killed by a Ugandan G-3 (308) that took him from behind and just clipped through the side of the neck, cutting his cephalic blood vessels on the right. Such a wound would deliver no shock, causing death by quick bleeding.

The Ugandans, such as they were, were using 308's, the pirates 30 R.S. (Kalashnikov), and the Israelis 9mm Parabellum. Of the five non-combatants who were killed, two were hit with Uzi's and three with AK's. This is a remarkably low tally considering the vast amount of hand-held automatic fire that was flying around.

Present at both actions and in command of one, Ulrich Wegener is now the senior counter-terror expert in the world. Even so he is still only an instrument of policy, and unless that policy is the right one no amount of technical and tactical brilliance will suffice to root out the evil once and for all. That the policy must be international is a very serious obstacle in a fragmented world, but it would seem to be a matter about which a fairly large consensus may be obtained.

Much as a local fiddler might ask Sarasati about violin techniques, I asked Colonel Wegener for his opinion about a set of principles I had drawn up to guide counter-terror activity. To my considerable delight we agreed on every point, thus:

A.   Terrorism must be stopped. It is generally successful at present so it is up to us to change that. The terrorist seeks to gain his point, to achieve notoriety, and—usually—to escape alive. We must deny him these objectives.

B.   Therefore, we must *never* grant him his demands, under any circumstances, at any price, though we may frequently *pretend* to acquiesce.

C.   Therefore, we must insure that no terrorist ever leaves the scene of his crime, unless dead or in custody.

D.   Therefore, we must insure that no terrorist is ever identified or publicized, neither personally nor by group or cause.

E.   Therefore, we must insure that, if taken alive, the terrorist is quickly punished by due process in proportion to his offense. This may call for "star chamber" courts repugnant to free societies, but we must choose the lesser of two evils.

F.   Therefore, we must seek maximum speed in responding to terrorist acts. They must be terminated before they can be advertised.

Colonel Wegener was pleased to relate an example of the last point. He was recently alerted to a possible terror hit inside Germany. (GSG 9 is directed to respond within one hour. In fact it is usually "wheels-up" in 15 minutes during working hours, and in 40 minutes when off duty.) A minister who was party to the alert came to the scene with all possible speed to observe the commando in action. Wegener met him as he arrived, to inform him that there was nothing to see since the episode was already over. You never heard about that one, did you? That is obviously the way to go!

In deriving tactical objectives from the foregoing principles we may note the following:

1.   Make sure that a terrorist action is really in operation.
2.   Act *quickly.*
3.   Prevent escape. (Live prisoners are not necessary.)
4.   Agree to anything. (What *color* helicopter?)
5.   Open an apparent exit. (Avoid the "cornered rat" syndrome.)
6.   Use whatever weapons are suitable. (Bio-chemical agents offer much promise.)
7.   Protect the innocent, if possible.

In a free society one cannot shut down publicity, but it is very desirable to conclude action before the press people show up. Anyone personally interested in any hostage must be excluded. The fate of the hostage must be held secondary to the fate of the perpetrator. This sounds callous, but terrorists who get away will strike again, and more people will die. We must bite the bullet.

The highly sophisticated GSG 9 does not publicize its tactics, for to do so would be to the advantage of the criminal, but its general skill level is most impressive. Every man is trained to do everything, and the atmosphere of dedication, comradeship, and pride is very apparent at the base. Wegener himself is a classic "up front" leader, and if he is not necessarily point man in every action, he is rarely more than a few steps behind. He tries every new technique himself, first, and at the age of 48 he is a spectacular athlete. At the time of my visit he was limping noticeably and I assumed that this was due to his wound at Entebbe. Actually it was the result of an in-motion truck dismount two days before.

I have certain ideas about the improvement of the commando's smallarms techniques which need not be dwelt upon here. Colonel Wegener will certainly acknowledge that nothing is so good that it cannot be improved. In this his viewpoint is both refreshing and inspiring, for the common police attitude is one of resistance to innovation. Counter-terror tactics frequently demand very careful marksmanship, combining extreme precision with decisive power. We have much to learn, and we are all hard at work.

If there is one thing about GSG 9 that provokes criticism—at least in Germany—it is cockiness. Young men belonging to a unit of this sort naturally think well of themselves—with very good cause. This may annoy some people, but it seems to me to be irrelevant. Pride may be viewed askance by Judeo-Christian theologians, but it is essential to the personality of a good soldier. The requisites of the fighting man are skill-at-arms, discipline, hardihood, valor, and pride. The absence of any single one of these components is fatal. Pride may be a sin to those who lack it, but it cannot be thought of negatively where force and violence are involved. It is amusing to hear a Nelson, a Custer, or a MacArthur derided as a "glory hunter." The pursuit of glory would certainly seem more respectable than the pursuit of votes, safety, or money. It is only when a man thinks that his title is enough—that it suffices to be a Marine, a Legionnaire, or a Guardsman—and forgets that it is up to him to live up to and aggrandize that appellation, that pride becomes a weakness. There seems to be little danger of that in GSG 9. Its men think they are good because they *are* good, and it would seem that as long as Wegener remains in command they will not be allowed to rest on their laurels.

Terrorism, like smallpox, must be eliminated—tossed into the garbage can of history along with the Inquisition, piracy, and the Black Death. It can be so eliminated if we so will, and the agencies of our will may well be organizations like GSG 9, and men like Ulrich Wegener.